ID0982972

Sweet Smoke
of
Rhetoric

A Collection of Renaissance Essays

UNIVERSITY OF MIAMI PUBLICATIONS

in

ENGLISH AND AMERICAN LITERATURE

NUMBER VII   JUNE 1964

Sweet Smoke
of
Rhetoric

A Collection of Renaissance Essays

Edited by

NATALIE GRIMES LAWRENCE

J. A. REYNOLDS

UNIVERSITY OF MIAMI PRESS

CORAL GABLES, FLORIDA

1964

v

The Arms of Sir Francis Drake

Sir Francis Drake (1545? - 1596) was the first Englishman to circumnavigate the world. Although the formal grant of arms was made by the Clarenceux King of Arms, reputedly Queen Elizabeth I designed arms and crest herself to commemorate his globe encircling achievement. The arms illustrate ocean stream between a heraldic version of the pole stars.

The crest is even more significant. It is Drake's own ship, the Golden Hind, escorted completely around the globe of earth by the hand of God.

Whether, as the story goes, the great Queen designed these arms or merely approved them, one thing is certain: she made a special trip to confer knighthood upon him on the deck of the very ship in which he had earned her favor. He had previously been termed an "upstart" by others of his name.

The blazon of his arms reads: "Sable, a fess wavy between two stars argent. Crest: a ship under reef, drawn round a terrestial globe with a cable by a hand issuing from clouds all proper."

The illustration was drawn by J. A. Reynolds for his book, *Heraldry and You: Modern Heraldic Usage in America.*

PR 423
.L3

Copyright 1964

by

University of Miami Press

Library of Congress Catalog Card Number: 64-17824

Printed in the United States of America

by

Atlantic Printers and Lithographers

Miami Beach, Florida

Preface

It is the nature of prefaces to have one virtue in common: they say what has to be said—and, more generally than not, with a minimum of beating the printer's devil about the bush; a merit, one notes, not always present in all that follows.

If a nation that does not honor its past has no future, even the smallest book, however spartan its pretentions, not honoring its sponsors, its contributors, and its well-wishers must share with its spiritual antitype no better fate than a most damnable life and deservéd death.

Though it seem somewhat late in history to concern ourselves unduly with the problems in scholarly delinquency that may have beset the perplexed academic constabulary in the old university town of Wittenberg, we might do well to avoid being hailed before the present courts of academic canon on the charge of having maltreated, with dentures sharper than a serpent's, the generous hands that fed us.

We stand amazed, as editors, before the abiding and simple faith of scholars, more especially the faith and patience of our colleagues who throughout many months accepted our suggestions, born of an arrogance inherent in the editorial status, for condensing, expanding, and revising their contributions. A belated honesty demands the admission that any defects in their articles must be attributed to our eternal meddling; all virtues, including the fabulous patience of Job, are theirs.

Their names appear in reasonably clear but inconspicuous type on the page of contents, each associated (not, perhaps, without auctorial misgivings) with the final version of title of each one's work after our months of badgering. But their names appear elsewhere, we believe, writ large in letters of gold and listed slightly higher than Abou Ben Adhem's.

It is traditionally the sorcerer's apprentice who stirs the brew. And the broth be not of his own making, and his name appear not on the label, it is he who in the complex mazes of the soft-pulp forest has helped to find and carry to the crucible those incredible mandrake roots that assume in the final distillate, for a day or for a decade, the charmed semblance of life. In his modern habit he generally retains his ancient anonymity; individually and severally he is the librarian. Though our

vii

AUG 31 1965

authors cannot thank him in their proper voices, we beg, like old Epilogue the Apologist, to do so for them. With appropriate protocol and thaumaturgy, and in the high epic tradition (if, indeed, we are not enroute to Wittigen Fair), we thus appreciatively catalogue his several names: Archie McNeal, Louis Morgan, George Rosner, Francis Langer, Madeline Riffey, Mildred Selle and all.

Now even Gloriana hath her true familiar, who, riding the distant winds, swoops like a merlin on her natural prey—the print shops of all Florida. We believe like Thomas, because we have seen, that Jane Gaffin of the University Press can stretch with her magic natural an impossibly slender budget into more book than that other Merlin with his darker arts.

But the glory of our University Press is Gloriana herself. It was, and is, Marjory Stoneman Douglas who conjured, not this volume alone, but the series of which it forms a part into a continuing reality. As Editor of the University of Miami Press she brings her scholarship, her enthusiasm, her sense of daring, and her engaging self into a field so often lacking in her exciting qualities. They have, as the literary world knows, long graced her careers as newspaperwoman, author, historian, and raconteuse.

And having violated as successfully as most others the well-established but seldom encountered natural attributes of prefaces, we remember, somewhat belatedly perhaps, that their ultimate nature is to end abruptly.

J. A. Reynolds

Coral Gables, Florida
May, 1963

About The Authors

James E. Wellington, B.A., M.A., Ph.D., is Associate Professor of English in the University of Miami. He has edited Alexander Pope's *Epistles to Several Persons (Moral Essays)* for the University of Miami Press.

William L. Halstead, B.A., M.A., Ph.D., is Professor of English and a member of the Graduate Faculty in the University of Miami. He is a recent contributor to the *Readers Companion to World Literature*, Dryden Press and Mentor Books. Dr. Halstead is also the author of *Shakespeare "Artistry and Artifice"*, University of Miami Press, forth coming publication.

John I. McCollum, Jr., B.A., M.A., Ph.D., is Associate Professor and Chairman of the Department of English in the University of Miami. He has contributed to the bibliographical studies of the Modern Humanities Research Association and is the editor of *The Age of Elizabeth* and *The Restoration Stage*.

Bruce E. Teets, B.A., M.A., Ph.D., is Associate Professor of English in the University of Miami. With the assistance of a small group of American and European scholars, he is currently editing and contributing to a complete annotated bibliography of writings about Joseph Conrad, to be published in *English Literature in Transition* and later in book form.

J. A. Reynolds, B.A., M.A., Ph.D., is a member of the Graduate Faculty and Professor of Medieval Language and Literature in the Department of English at the University of Miami. He is the author and illustrator of *Heraldry and You*, Thomas Nelson and Sons, New York; co-editor of and contributor to *A Chaucerian Puzzle and Other Medieval Essays*, University of Miami Press, Coral Gables, Florida.

Natalie Grimes Lawrence, A.B., M.A., is Professor of English and Humanities at the University of Miami. She is the author of a number of studies in Shakespeare and other Renaissance writers, and was co-editor of and contributor to *A Chaucerian Puzzle and other Medieval Essays*, No. V of University of Miami Publications in English and American Literature.

CONTENTS

SWEET SMOKE OF RHETORIC
A Collection of Renaissance Essays

Introduction

The title of this volume implies acceptance of the term *Renaissance*. Yet the editors are not unaware that this term has been sharply questioned in the twentieth century—even repudiated—as not inclusive of the manifold activity of the time-span indicated: roughly, the three hundred years or more including Petrarch and Jonson, classicists both.

Fourteenth century scholars in Italy were notable in realizing the period in which they were living. For, rejoicing in the Latin, they thought of themselves as men of the *Renascentia*: those reborn into a greater conception of man's potential through renewed study of the Greek and Roman classics and the further discovery of manuscrips forgotten in the dust of ages. Something of the high belief of these men of letters comes to us untarnished from Petrarch's account of his finding in the Cathedral Library at Verona a manuscript containing the sixteen books of Cicero's letters *Ad Atticum*, three books of *Ad Quintum* and two of *Ad Brutum*.

Nearly a hundred years had passed after the death of Ben Jonson before the English began to employ the term Renascence (1727) to signify the period of the rebirth of classical studies. Another hundred years or so later, England borrowed from France the term *Renaissance* which gradually supplanted Renascence. Then our century, about thirty years ago, began to have misgivings. Actually we were not the pioneers in these questionings that we have sometimes been assumed to be. Pater, Symonds, and Burckhardt before them in the 1860 Basle edition of his *The Civilization of the Renaissance in Italy*, all felt and expressed some of the limitations of the term, yet fully used it. In 1961, Denys Hay in his introduction reconsiders both the hazard and validity of using the term, but he calls his excellent work, *The Italian Renaissance in its Historical Backgrounds*.

In the third quarter of the twentieth century, it seems appropriate that we take a mild tranquilizer in the thought that a term is a symbol, not a complete description and remember that man is lost in dealing with time until he can do it up into parcels, neatly, albeit inaccurately, labeled. For such label acts as a guide to his whereabouts in time as the astrolabe served Columbus to determine his latitude in the long reaches of the Atlantic.

What comprised the *Renaissance* we shall keep on trying to perceive as our researches continue and as our comprehension of the growing body of knowledge of the period allows us to apprehend it more fully. What it means to many of us today is ever a self-renewing question. First one wants to answer: an infinite variety. It still means a revived faith in the importance and dignity of man such as Pico and Beatus Rhenanus envisaged; it means man's hunger for learning of differing kinds, his curiosity about himself and his universe. Copernicus dared, privately at least, to theorize that the earth is not the center of the universe but the sun and that the earth revolves about it. In the heliocentric theory Copernicus, influenced by the followers of the Greek Pythagorus, laid the foundation of modern astronomy. Bruno deducing in his prison cell a universe made up not of one world but an infinite number of worlds is like Hamlet who, though bounded in a nutshell, would count himself king of an infinite space. The phrase is the same in Bruno and Shakespeare, significantly.

Grotius, analyzing man as a sociable creature needing to live in peace and order with his fellows, came to the conclusion that "the Mother of Civil Laws is Obligation by mutual compact and since mutual compact derives its force from Natural Law, Nature may be said to be the Grandmother of Civil Laws." The statement is Greek in spirit, homely as parts of the *Iliad* and bears within it the renewed concentration upon man as himself worthy of respect as a natural creature and furthermore a responsible being. Yet to the somewhat earlier Machiavelli and the later Hobbes, man whether prince or pauper is an opportunist.

Renaissance curiosity about the universe also evidenced itself as a desire for the perilous but perhaps rewarding navigation of air and sea. Probably the first man after Icarus to believe flight practicable by other than necromantic means was Leonardi da Vinci. Sixteenth century designs and manuscripts of his, buried for more than three hundred years, reveal his understanding of mechanical problems involved in flying and remain as pathfinders in man's hope to penetrate space. Immediately useful were the experiments of Galileo in the early seventeenth century involving the telescope so that by 1610 he was able to locate and describe the satellites of Jupiter.

As soon as the first years of the fifteenth century, men were attempting new routes to the Orient, whether for trade or incidental conquest. Since the voyages of the Polo family, Venice had held complete control of the rich trade over the Mediterranean and caravan route to the Far East. But Portuguese mariners under Henry the Navigator sought another sea-lane by way of Africa. However, not until well after Henry's death did Bartholomeu Diaz, in 1486, round the Cape of Good Hope. In

1497, Vasco da Gama sailed down the Tagus past Lisbon to the African shore; circled its whole south coast; and, in the following May, arrived at Calicut. His first cargo of spices from India broke the Venetian monopoly. One recalls that the Genoese Columbus had sailed hopefully westward for India from Palos, Spain in 1492. The sixteenth century English learned to build ships more maneuverable than ever before which became tools in the race to find a Northwest Passage to India or Cathay but also cut the waters toward a Northeast Passage to that same Cathay. Francis Drake, joining the search for new trade routes, almost by the way, became the first to girdle the earth, though unlike Puck, not in eighty minutes. He too rounded the Cape of Good Hope, returning to England to kneel upon the quarter deck of his sturdy ship the *Golden Hind* to receive the accolade of knighthood from the Queen.

The old had not entirely receded for the new. Man clung to his religion—more than was at one time thought—feeling himself, as Banquo testifies, "in the great hand of God." To be sure there was often yearning to change the forms of religion but also stiff opposition to such change. Erasmus, loyal Catholic that he was, yet longed more than he did to sport with praise of folly to do away with the increasingly involved churchly government and to return, even as Petrarch wished, to the profound simplicity of the Christ of the Gospels. Luther at last broke away from Mother Church, and Calvin set up new Institutions. But alas! the Inquisitions waxed and waned over the years, too many years. Rabelais was a monk, though hardly a devout one; Petrarch and Copernicus were canons; John Donne became the greatest of English Divines. Marlowe though accused of atheism did not die for it, bitter as the accusations were. However, a few years later Bruno was burned at the stake as a heretic. Yet Michelangelo painting the frescoes of the Sistine Chapel had shown in the *Creation of Adam*, God just laying a finger on his magnificent creature man.

It is impossible in a brief introduction to convey in nice proportion the extent and reach of this period, but to some, at least, the sweet fruition of its earthly crown is in the Arts. From Giotto to Raphael the Italian painters astound and feast the eye of the beholder with color. In Italy, the Netherlands, Spain the new perspective supplants the former linearity; portraiture assumes the look of life itself. Brunelleschi's dome atop the Cathedral at Florence and Michelangelo's at St. Peter's place architecture solidly within the classical revival. Even Christopher Wren wanted a dome for St. Paul's and got it but only after concessions to his Bishops whose intent was for Gothic spires. The anonimity of the artist in the centuries immediately preceding came to a slow halt; the artist recognized as an individual now, sometimes, signed his work—though not customarily. In the churches, in the statues of the great tombs, in the palaces, one thinks of size and grandeur; but the small and exquisite had also honored place, from the goldsmith's art to the miniatures. Benvenuto's salt cellar is a notable diminishing from the panels of Ghiberti's North and East doors of the Baptistry in Florence, but the goldsmith's craft is basic to each. Nicholas Hilliard the English miniaturist was the son of a goldsmith and worked in his father's shop. This training in shaping and graving is beautifully evident in his miniatures, as for instance his *Young Man in Deep Mourning* with its clean lines subduing what ornamentation there is. The work of Jean Clouet in France and that of the French Huegonot, Oliver Isaac, in London, testify to the appreciation of the miniature by Renaissance taste. Especially interesting for its connection with literature is the miniature by Oliver Isaac of Sir Philip Sidney in pastoral garb. Many others lent their talents to this art, Holbein becoming supreme in it during his second residence in England.

The usual stress upon the growth of nationalism in this period has seemed to scant an accompanying development of a new kind of internationalism. The curiosity of man concerning himself tended to broaden to an inclusion of other times and other lands. Granted that this internationalism continued to depend, as formerly, upon the scholars' knowledge of Latin, increasingly it drew upon their familiarity with Greek and the vernacular tongues. Especially by the efforts of the translators as well as those of scholars, the printed word became polylingual. From Boccaccio's translation of six books of the *Iliad* to the anonymous rendering into English of the *Decameron*, published by Jaggard in 1620, a steadily industrious army of translators made western man conscious of more than one nation's thought in greater degree than before; in fact, the influence of these translations upon individual men in showing them that they were integers in a family of nations has hardly been adequately evaluated even to the present time.

However, the historians, and sometimes the translators, saw to it that Renaissance man should be proud to consider himself a part of his own nation. Despite the many city states, Biondo in *Italia Illustrata* proposed to write a history of Italy, Guicchiardini did so in the great *Storia d'Italia*. Britain which from the Anglo-Saxon Chronicle had been writing British history quickened and multiplied these accounts. Polydore Vergil, Holinshed, Harrison, Hall, Stowe, and Philemon Holland's translation of Camden's *Britannia* all bear witness, as do likewise the chronicle plays, to a revived interest in national history. On the other hand, Lord Berner's translation of *The Chronicles of Froissart*, North's Plutarch, and

Florio's translation from the Italian version of Cartier's *Two Navigations* point, except for the countries whose histories are incidentally involved, away from rather than toward nationalism. Furthermore internationalism is at least latent in the ebullient spirit of those historians who felt confidant to write a history not merely of a nation but of the world: one example must suffice, Sir Walter Raleigh composing his *History of the World* while confined in the Tower of London.

Actually one pauses to wonder whether the philosophers of the Renaissance were more native or classic; for Plato, Aristotle, Plotinus, and Seneca were as present in thought as Pico, Ficino, Vives, or Bacon, different as the point of view of the Renaissance thinkers might be from their classic predecessors.

The music of this time-span, while showing clear indebtedness to Medieval chant and motet becomes lighter-hearted or more secularly sad. From Josquin des Prez and Palestrina (not forgetting Dufay, Ockheghem, and Obrecht) to Bird, Morley, and Weelkes in England, the music worked its contrapuntal sorcery, "haling the soul out of men's bodies", as Shakespeare knew.

Yet there are those of us to whom the Renaissance is primarily a literary movement emerging by a rebirth of the classics into an idiom essentially its own. Just as to the student of literature, the very sight of his books upon the shelves delights him, the names of the writers of this period awake memories of their power in prose and poetry: Petrarch, Boccaccio, Ariosto; Ronsard, DuBellay, Montaigne; Cervantes; Erasmus, Sir Thomas More, Spenser, Sidney, Marlowe, Shakespeare, Donne, Jonson. The list is significant in its omissions, but a small part of it has been sufficient to provide focus for this volume.

Natalie Grimes Lawrence

Coral Gables, Florida
May 9, 1963

James E. Wellington

Part 1

RENAISSANCE ANTI-FEMINISM AND THE CLASSICAL TRADITION[1]

A widespread assumption has long been current among students of Renaissance poetry that the strain of anti-feminism which appears so prominently in the lyric verse of the sixteenth and seventeenth centuries can be explained quite simply as a calculated rebellion against the Petrarchan love-longing.[2] According to this belief, the sophomoric extravagances of the Petrarchan lover, with his

> . . . boddye all wrislye, the collor pale and wan,
> More like a gost than lyk a lyving man,[3]

began to pall upon Renaissance lyric poets as early as Wyatt, with the result that a marked reaction against the Petrarchan complaint gradually began to assert itself. Accordingly (so the theory runs), among their patently Petrarchan lyrics these poets began to mingle poems which embodied a more manly and independent attitude toward love and woman— an attitude, in fact, which often became downright hostile. Such a hypothesis provides a simple and eminently plausible explanation for the change which occurred in love poetry from the querulous death-wish of the Tudor sonneteers to the cynical independence of their seventeenth-century successors. For an established (and greatly overworked) poetic conven-

1

tion the theory substitutes its opposite, saying, in effect, that if a slavish and spaniel-like devotion to a scornful mistress is Petrarchism, the libertine harangue against that same lady must be anti-Petrarchism, that is, an attack on the Petrarchan convention.

There is a measure of truth in this theory; and yet, in view of the tremendous complexity of the forces which shaped the poetry of the Renaissance, it seems just a bit too simple. I think that such an oversimplification tends to exaggerate the importance which the Renaissance poet ascribed to the theme of his poem, that it unaccountably neglects the obvious thematic conventionality of much lyric poetry of the period. The theory obscures the possibility that anti-feminism in Renaissance poetry may well be in itself a convention instead of a reaction against one. It obscures the fact that there actually exists in Renaissance poetry a genuine and valid anti-Petrarchism which is neither conventional nor anti-feministic. And, further, it obscures the fact that libertine anti-feminism in the Renaissance must be attributed in great measure to the fondness of Renaissance poets for imitating the themes of Greek and Latin verse.

Anti-feminism, for the purposes of this discussion, does not refer to the wholesale denunciation of woman as tempter, seducer, and shrew, the cause of all man's troubles since the Fall. It is rather the angry remonstrance of a man who has courted a lady and been either jilted or scornfully refused. Thus injured, the poet warns his lady that in neglecting a perfectly good opportunity for love she is making a serious mistake; for the day is not far distant (he predicts) when her vaunted beauty will be gone, when she who in the bloom of youth so coldly refused to grant her favors will be just as coldly rejected in her turn, withered, ugly, and alone. The contrast is vividly illustrated in Renaissance painting in two canvases by Giorgione: his voluptuous *Sleeping Venus* and his bitter portrait of an aged woman holding in one hand the motto *Col tempo* ("with Time") and pointing sadly with the other to her own wrinkled countenance as an example of the ravages of time and old age on feminine beauty. Some poems on the subject are more brutal than others, and some are addressed to the female sex in general instead of to an individual. Occasionally the person speaking in the poem is not himself the lover but argues on behalf of another (as does Pandarus to Criseyde, for example, in Chaucer's *Troilus and Criseyde,* lines 393-406) or in favor of sexual promiscuity as a general principle (as Corisca does in Guarini's *Il Pastor Fido*). Sometimes, too, the exhortation is to marriage rather than to illicit love; and in some poems the admonition is to a boy rather than to a girl. But most often the poet himself is adopting the pose of a rejected lover, reproaching the object of his unrequited passion for her cruelty and shortsightedness in spurning his advances. In the wicked lines of Thomas Carew,

> When beauty, youth, and all sweets leave her,
> Love may return, but lover never:
> And old folks say there are no pains
> Like itch of love in aged veins.[4]
> ("To A. L.: Persuasions to Love," lines 65-68)

This is the very antithesis of the Petrarchan complaint. From the lofty pedestal on which the triple cult of courtly love, Petrarchism, and Renaissance neo-Platonism had placed her, woman has been unceremoniously pulled down and shown to be made of matter, to be subject to all the ugly and destructive processes of material decay. She is no longer the divine wellspring of spiritual inspiration but a mere sexual partner, a material object to be temporarily possessed. If this is all she is, her loss is no longer an occasion for mourning but a source of irritation and even rage. It is consequently not for the frustrated lover to worship from afar, to pine and weep and wish to die; it is rather for him to denounce, and often to jeer, the proud and scornful beauty who will not have him. This is Renaissance anti-feminism to the core, and it is admittedly the exact opposite of Petrarchism.

Two difficulties, however, now arise. The first is that a poetic theme which is the opposite of Petrarchism is not necessarily a revolt against it and cannot without great difficulty be proved such. Second, this so-called anti-Petrarchism is older by many centuries than either Petrarch or the poetic convention which customarily bears his name. In some ways it exemplifies once more man's age-old recognition of his own mortality and is therefore (as I have argued elsewhere) a variant of the *carpe diem* theme.[5] It is close to the Biblical reminder, found in both the Old Testament and the New, that flesh is grass, that beauty is ephemeral, that all the glories of the world around us are doomed to wither away.[6] Moreover, it is a commonplace of Greek and Latin lyric and elegiac verse, from which (as this discussion will presently show) it passed into the love poetry of the Renaissance and would probably have done so had Petrarch never written a single sonnet to Laura of the golden hair.

The Greco-Roman world recognized a deity who, according to varying accounts, was responsible for igniting the spark of reciprocal love or exacting vengeance for unrequited love, both of which are problems relevant to the present discussion. The name of this god was Anteros, and he is usually identified in the literature of antiquity as brother to Eros and son to Aphrodite.[7] Although his name etymologically suggests that he was in some sense a foil or *alter ego* to his mischievous brother, the exact nature of his function with regard to earthly lovers is difficult to ascertain with precision. The dual character of the responsibilities commonly attributed to Anteros indicates that he must have been a somewhat shadowy figure even to the ancients, and the problem is clouded further by still other interpretations which both the ancient world and the Renaissance occasionally placed on this peculiar and elusive deity.[8] Nevertheless, the two functions of Anteros outlined above appear from the late Professor Merrill's study of the problem to have been both real and significant to classical and Renaissance poet alike, and a rejected lover might well appeal to the god on either count. Our present concern is with Anteros as *deus ultor*, avenger of love disprized; for it is necessary to understand that vengeance of this nature was regarded seriously in the ancient world. This role Anteros appears to have fulfilled at Athens, according to a first-hand report from Pausanias. While in Athens, Pausanias saw an altar erected to Anteros in his capacity as the avenger of slighted love:

> The altar within the city called the altar of Anteros (*Love Avenged*) they say was dedicated by the resident aliens, because the Athenian Meles, spurning the love of Timagoras, a resident alien, bade him ascend to the highest point of the rock and cast himself down. Now Timagoras took no account of his life, and was ready to gratify the youth in any of his requests, so he went and cast himself down. When Meles saw that Timagoras was dead, he suffered such pangs of remorse that he threw himself from the same rock and so died. From this time the resident aliens worshipped as Anteros the avenging spirit of Timagoras.[9]
>
> (*Description of Greece* i. 30. 1)

What Pausanias saw commemorated a punishment of some severity, but the underlying principle is quite clear—that capricious cruelty on the part of one who is loved without loving in return is intolerable and must be avenged. As Wyatt was to write many centuries later,

> Vengaunce shall fall on thy disdain,
> That makest but game on ernest pain.[10]

The vengeance invoked by Wyatt on his disdainful mistress is not violent death but loss of beauty, a punishment conventional in this kind of poetry; but the difference is only one of degree. The real question for the literary historian is whether a Renaissance poet who calls for such punishment is rebelling against Petrarch or merely echoing a common-place of Greek and Latin poetry. The fact that vengeance for the slights of unrequited love was important enough in Athens to merit the inter-cession of a deity and the erection of an altar strongly suggests its pos-sible use as a theme in poetry as well—a theme, be it said, which must have been in existence many centuries before anyone could possibly have rebelled against Petrarch.

And so it was. The great antiquity of the supposedly anti-Petrarchan attack on the haughty and unyielding lover is attested by the frequency with which it occurs in the Greek Anthology and the Roman elegists. Consider, for example, the following epigram made by Julianus, prefect of Egypt, in the reign of Justinian:

> Charming Maria is too exalted: but do thou, holy Justice, punish her arrogance, yet not by death, my Queen, but on the contrary may she reach grey old age, may her hard face grow wrinkled. May the grey hairs avenge these tears, and beauty, the cause of her soul's transgression, suffer for it.[11]
> (*The Greek Anthology* v. 298)

This bitter imprecation, as Professor Hutton has pointed out, was imitated in French by Ronsard, Maynard, and Jean de la Péruse, and in Latin by Joseph Justus Scaliger.[12] Ronsard's imitation enlarges considerably (as Ronsard often did) upon the original, but it contains all the elements of vengeance found in Julianus' poem, including the prayer for old age as a fate worse than death:

> Je ne veux point la mort de celle qui arreste
> Mon cœur en sa prison; mais, Amour pour venger
> Mes larmes de six ans, fay ses cheveux changer,
> Et seme bien espais des neiges sur sa teste.
>   Si tu veux, la vengeance est desja toute preste:
> Tu accourcis les ans, tu les peux allonger.
> Ne souffres en ton camp ton soudart outrager.
> Que vieille elle devienne, ottroyant ma requeste.
>   Elle se glorifie en ses cheveux frisez.
> En sa verde jeunesse, en ses yeux aiguisez,
> Qui tirent dans les cœurs mille pointes encloses.
>   Pourquoy te braves-tu de cela qui n'est rien?
> La beauté n'est que vent, la beauté n'est pas bien,
> Les beautez en un jour s'en-vont comme les roses.[13]
> (*Sonnets pour Helene*, I, 62)

This sonnet, like the others in the Hélène group, was addressed to the beautiful valetudinarian Hélène de Surgères, whom Ronsard had met and unsuccessfully wooed in the *précieux* salon of the maréchale de Retz

in 1570.[14] Hélène was absolutely unattainable—delicate in health, reso-
lutely neo-Platonic in her attitude toward love, and (Professor Bishop
implies) emotionally frigid into the bargain—and the poem pours forth
all of Ronsard's resentment and frustration in the face of a hopeless love
affair. Classicist that he was, he turned to the Greek Anthology, which,
as he well knew, abounds in cries for vengeance on coldhearted and in-
accessible boys and girls. He found the epigram of Julianus; and, as Hutton further suggests, he may have had in mind another poem from the
Anthology as well, an epigram from the collection known as *Musa
Puerilis* (Book xii).[15] This collection of epigrams is largely the work
of Strato of Sardis, and the present epigram is Strato's:

> If thou gloriest in thy beauty, know that the rose too
> blooms, but withers of a sudden and is cast away on the
> dunghill. To blossom and to beauty the same time is allotted,
> and envious time withers both together.[16]
> (*The Greek Anthology* xii. 234)

Aside from the use of *glory* as a verb (Fr. *elle se glorifie*; Gk. *kauchā*),
the two poems have only the commonplace of the withering rose to
connect them textually. It can therefore not be demonstrated, and
Hutton does not insist, that Strato's epigram was beyond any doubt
a source for Ronsard's sonnet. Nevertheless, the possibility plainly exists.
And the similarity between Ronsard's sonnet and the other epigram, that
by Julianus, is remarkably close. All three poems, in fact, are thematically
alike; and the very existence of Strato's epigram, whether Ronsard used
it or not, serves to emphasize further the fondness of the poets of the
Anthology for invoking the punishment of time and old age upon a
haughty charmer. Although the theme of Ronsard's sonnet is just the
opposite of the humble supplication of the Petrarchan lover, the evidence
for its anti-Petrarchan provenance is far less strong than that for its origin
in the Greek Anthology.

An equally bitter epigram from the Anthology is the following by
Rufinus:

> Rhodope is exalted by her beauty, and if I chance to say
> "Good day," salutes me only with her proud eyebrows. If I
> ever hang garlands over her door, she crushes them under her
> haughty heels in her wrath. Come quickly, wrinkles, and pit-
> iless old age; make haste. Do you at least unbend Rhodope.[17]
> (*The Greek Anthology* v. 92)

Hutton has found no fewer than twelve Renaissance adaptations of
this epigram in France and the Netherlands alone.[18] Among them is the
following passage from Joannes Secundus:

Nam tibi quod prosit faciem corrumpere rugis?
    Hae venient fronti, nec mora longa, tuae.
Quin potius, dum fata sinunt et nigra sororum
    Stamina, verque viret nobile, carpe rosas.[19]

(Elegia, I, v. 11-14)

As another possible source for Secundus' elegy Hutton suggests Ovid
Ars Amatoria ii. 115-120; but the important thing to notice is that Secundus' cynical acceptance of reality need not be taken as a specific rebellion against Petrarchan idealism. It is a distinct echo of a poetic convention from classical antiquity.

    A less malicious epigram by this same Rufinus utters a similar warning of imminent old age:

> I send thee this garland, Rhodoclea, that with my own hands
> I wove out of beautiful flowers. There are lilies and roses and
> dewy anemones, and tender narcissus and purple-gleaming vio-
> lets. Wear it and cease to be vain. Both thou and the garland
> flower and fade.[20]

(The Greek Anthology v. 74)

This poem, according to the catalogue of Professor Hutton, was imitated by Renaissance poets in France and the Netherlands no fewer than nineteen times, and the list includes both a sonnet and an elegy by Ronsard. In each of these poems Ronsard follows Rufinus in offering the example of a bouquet or garland, gathered and woven by the poet's own hand, as a warning that the lady's beauty will prove quite as fleeting as the beauty of the flowers. Here is the sonnet:

>   Je vous envoye un bouquet que ma main
> Vient de trier de ces fleurs épanies;
> Qui ne les eust à ce vespre cueillies,
> Cheutes à terre elles fussent demain.
>   Cela vous soit un example certain,
> Que vos beautez, bien qu'elles soient fleuries,
> En peu de tems cherront toutes fletries,
> Et, comme fleurs, periront tout soudain.
>   Le tems s'en va, le tems s'en va, ma Dame,
> Las! le tems non, mais nous nous en allons,
> Et tost serons estendus sous la lame,
>   Et des amours, desquelles nous parlons,
> Quand serons morts, n'en sera plus nouvelle:
> Pource aimez moy, cependant qu'estes belle.[22]

(Continuations des Amours, 1555)

Ronsard's second poem on this subject, his Elegie XI, provides the very same warning in greatly expanded form, and the note of vengeance in the elegy rings out venomous and clear—a good deal more so, in fact, than in the more reflective and sorrowful sonnet. Both the sonnet and the elegy are, by their very nature, more discursive than the epigram of Rufinus, but the evidence is nevertheless very strong that the so-called anti-Petrarchism of these two poems may well derive from Rufinus and that it is far older than Petrarch and his followers.

The epigrams thus far cited from the Greek Anthology are only a few of many similar expressions of anti-feminism with which the Anthology abounds.[24] Since these poems were not scurrilous enough to have been excluded from the bowdlerized collection of Maximus Planudes, the only edition of the Anthology known to Ronsard and his contemporaries, it is certain that they were familiar to scholars and poets in the Renaissance, either from the Planudean Anthology itself or (for those who had small Greek) through Latin intermediaries. But the important fact to notice at this juncture is that the so-called anti-Petrarchan attack on the scornful or dilatory mistress is a common theme among the amatory epigrams of the Greek Anthology, that Renaissance poets were well aware of its existence there, and that many Renaissance expressions of this theme can be traced with no difficulty whatever to Greek sources and (as will be seen) to Latin sources as well.

Libertine anti-feminism in antiquity is by no means confined to Greek lyric. The poetry of Ovid, during the Renaissance one of the most popular and widely imitated of Latin poets, presents notable instances of the anti-feministic harangue. The lines from Ovid cited above in connection with Secundus (*Ars Amatoria ii.* 115-120) are relatively mild, but there is a longer passage in the same work (iii. 59-80) which is quite another matter. Here Ovid objectifies the passing of time in a remarkable variety of images, all of which were to become standard weapons in the Renaissance struggle against feminine frigidity: the withering of blossoms, the flowing of water, the ability of snakes to shed their skins and of stags to renew their antlers (woman, of course, cannot thus rejuvenate herself)—all for the purpose of exhorting young women in vivid and frightening terms to seize the ecstasy of love before their beauty fades forever. It is instructive to compare this passage with Carew's "To A. L.: Persuasions to Love," four very un-Petrarchan lines from which have already been quoted in this discussion; for Carew says so many of the same things in so many of the same ways that one is tempted to suspect a direct borrowing. It is true that Ovid is not himself a rejected lover here; in keeping with the spirit of the poem as a whole, his warning is addressed to young women in general rather than to an individual. But his cruel reminder of the transience of feminine beauty is quite in the tradition of what was to become Renaissance anti-feminism; it would be regarded by a Petrarchan suppliant as a bitter and heretical doctrine. Other instances of this cynical attitude are to be found not only in Ovid himself but in the other Roman elegists, Propertius and Tibullus; and in Catullus, Vergil, Horace, and Martial—sufficient evidence, one would suppose, of the extent to which this argument was invoked in the poetry of classical Rome.[25]

The widespread incidence of the rebellious lover in Greek and Roman poetry implies, therefore, as a working hypothesis, the clear possibility that poets of the sixteenth and seventeenth centuries may well have derived the theme in great measure from ancient sources, and the hypothesis is borne out by the numerous similarities thus far noted between classical and Renaissance expressions of this theme. Some of the similarities, of course, are closer and more detailed than others and carry somewhat greater conviction accordingly, although none, I believe, are entirely negligible. The hypothesis is further strengthened, moreover, by a remarkable chain of four poems, comprising not only translation but translation of translation, beginning in the reign of the emperor Augustus and ending in that of Charles II. These poems will make it possible to trace the so-called anti-Petrarchism of Renaissance anti-feminism in a virtually unbroken line over a stretch of some sixteen hundred years, from the classical period to the mid-seventeenth century, with no necessary stopovers at Petrarchan way stations.

The first of these poems is Horace's ode to Ligurinus (*Odes* iv. 10), beginning, "O crudelis adhuc, et Veneris muneribus potens," a poem which bears an obvious thematic resemblance to the selections from the Greek Anthology already mentioned. Here the poet declares that, although today Ligurinus is proud and scornful in the possession of his charms, the evidence of his mirror (a common piece of equipment in this kind of poetry) will one day cause him to regret his arrogance and the opportunities for love which he has wasted. The concluding lines embody the poet's warning that Ligurinus will then know in all its sadness "the itch of love in aged veins," and he will ask himself disconsolately,

> Quae mens est hodie, cur eadem non puero fuit?
> Vel cur his animis incolumes non redeunt genæ?[26]

The poet, in other words, is predicting that when old age has ruined Ligurinus' youthful beauty he will say (roughly translated), "Why, as a boy, did I not feel the way I feel today? Or why, since now I feel this way, do not my rosy cheeks return unharmed?" Pride goeth before destruction—in this case, the destruction of the lad's happiness as well as his beauty; and this is the very argument commonly described as anti-Petrarchan when it appears in the poetry of the Renaissance.

Now this ode of Horace, as Sainte-Beuve pointed out,[27] has been imitated in French by Ronsard, in an ode beginning, "Jeune beauté, mais trop outrecuidée" (*Odes*, III, 13, "A sa maistresse"). Ronsard expands the original (as we have seen him do elsewhere) to twenty-eight lines, addresses it to a girl instead of to a boy, and adds a note of vengeful vindictiveness lacking in Horace's ode; but the basic similarity between the two is otherwise very strong. In Ronsard's version, for example, the last two lines of Horace's Latin quoted above appear as follows:

> Que ne pensoy-je alors que j'estoy belle
> Ce que je vay pensant?
> Ou bien, pourquoy à mon desir pareille
> Ne suis-je maintenant?[28]
>
> (Lines 7-10)

Further, Ronsard's opening lines closely parallel—indeed, virtually translate—the first line of Horace's ode:

> *Horace:* O crudelis adhuc, et Veneris muneribus potens;
> *Ronsard:* Jeune beauté, mais trop outrecuidée
> Des presens de Venus.

That portion of Ronsard's passage which follows the comma is a faithful rendition of Horace's "et Veneris muneribus potens"; only in his "Jeune beauté" does Ronsard depart from the original Latin. And the theme is identical in both poems. Ronsard's ode, in short, is a clear example of Renaissance anti-feminism which originates not in anti-Petrarchism but in a specific classical source.

Ronsard's ode, in its turn, has been imitated by Thomas Stanley (1625-1678), the English poet, classical scholar, and translator of the Anacreontea. Stanley's poem, entitled "The Revenge: Ronsard," adheres to the theme of vengeance inaugurated by Horace's ode and preserved by Ronsard, but he compresses Ronsard's French (his immediate model) into three quatrains, as follows:

> Fair Rebell to thy selfe, and Time,
> Who laughst at all my tears,
> When thou hast lost thy youthful prime
> And age his Trophie rears,
>
> Weighing thy inconsiderate pride
> Thou shalt in vain accuse it,

> Why Beauty am I now deni'd
> 　　Or knew not then to use it?
>
> Then shall I wish, ungentle Fair
> 　　Thou in like flames may'st burn;
> Venus, if just, will hear my prayer
> 　　And I shall laugh my turn.[29]
> 　　　　(*Poems*, 1651)

Note that lines 7-10 of Ronsard's ode (quoted above)—his rendering of the last two lines of Horace's ode to Ligurinus—appear, much condensed, as lines 7-8 of Stanley's poem:

> Why Beauty am I now deni'd
> 　　Or knew not then to use it?

George Saintsbury believed that Stanley was imitating Ronsard's famous sonnet (on the same subject) beginning "Quand vous serez bien vieille, le soir à la chandelle" (*Sonnets pour Helene*, XLIII), but Saintsbury appears to have been guessing.[30] Mario Praz has since given proof that Stanley had in mind the Ronsard ode under discussion here.[31] Several close parallels, in addition to the one cited, bear out Praz's view, and the last of these brings Horace into the matter once again. In a poem (*Epodes* 15) which otherwise does not quite fit this discussion, Horace cries vengeance on a successful male rival by saying that when the fickle Neæra shall desert the latter as she has already deserted Horace, "ast ego vicissim risero" ("But I in turn shall laugh"). Ronsard borrows this line, the last line of Horace's fifteenth epode, as the last line of his own ode "A sa maistresse," under discussion here: "Je me rie à mon tour," a literal tranlation of Horace's Latin. And a glance at Stanley's imitation of Ronsard quoted above reveals his concluding line to be "And I shall laugh my turn," a literal translation of Ronsard's French. Ronsard and Stanley, of course, are addressing a scornful mistress rather than a successful rival for her favors, and their use of Horace's line is therefore somewhat different from his. Nevertheless, the three lines are the same, and they serve to emphasize further the link which binds Renaissance anti-feminism with its source in the literature of antiquity.

In all three of these poems—Horace's ode to Ligurinus, Ronsard's ode "A sa maistress," and Stanley's "The Revenge: Ronsard"—the theme is the vindictive warning that when youthful beauty has withered to old age and the cruel charmer is no longer sexually desirable, she (or he) will bitterly repent her scorn. When the three are taken together, they provide a very cogent example of the persistence of libertine anti-feminism from the age of Augustus to the mid-seventeenth century without necessary reference either to Petrarchism or to reactions against it.

One final link in the chain is afforded by a direct translation of Horace's ode to Ligurinus from the pen of the Restoration poet and painter Thomas Flatman (1637-1688), whose version is entitled "To Ligurinus, a beauteous Youth."

> 'Tis true, thou art yet fair, my Ligurine,
> No down as yet environs cheek or chin:
> But when those hairs which now do flow, shall fall,
> And when thy rosy cheeks turn wan and pale:
> When in thy glass another Ligurine thou
> Shalt spy, and scarce thy bearded self shalt know;
> Then thou (despis'd) shalt sing this piteous song;
> Why am I old? or why was every young?[32]

Flatman's poem (which does justice to his name if not to Horace) is manifestly unworthy of the intellectual subtleties of the original, nor can it match the music and the vitality of Ronsard's adaptation. Still, the very fact that it exists at all is further evidence that the persistence of the rebellious lover in sixteenth and seventeenth-century poetry cannot be entirely explained by an anti-Petrarchan revolution. The classical influence must be accorded its fair share of the responsibility.

A great deal of further evidence might easily be adduced to support the contention that the classical influence on sixteenth and seventeenth-century lyric has been insufficiently regarded as a source of the rebellious-lover theme. Robert Burton, for example, as part of his cure for love-melancholy, invokes some fifty-five Greek and Latin authorities to demonstrate the perishability and consequent worthlessness of feminine charm, and he includes portraits of feminine decrepitude that would make a convinced Petrarchan squirm.[33] When Robert Herrick calls down the vengeance of time and old age upon a frigid mistress—as he does, for example, in "To Myrrha Hardhearted" and in "The Changes, to Corinna"—the careful reader hears many an echo of Propertius and Tibullus, to say nothing of the Greek Anthology.[34] When Sir Robert Ayton (1570-1638), giving the theme a slightly different twist, heartlessly compares the ruined beauty of an unchaste woman to that of a rose which has been promiscuously handled ("To His Forsaken Mistress"),[35] he is using an image identical with that in the second epithalamium of Catullus (*Carmina* 62. 39-47), one of the authorities cited by Burton. Or perhaps Ayton is following a passage in Ariosto (*Orlando Furioso*, i. 42-43), which is a direct imitation of the same passage in the second epithalamium of Catullus. Or perhaps he had in mind the William Byrd madrigal "La Verginella," which is modeled upon the Ariosto passage. And the very same metaphor to which Catullus has given such currency may be seen at least twice in the Greek Anthology, in an epigram by Philippus of Thessalonica and in one by Rufinus as well.[36]

In all the instances mentioned, the theme of the rebellious lover can be traced without interruption or divergence all the way back to the poetry of classical antiquity, a literary genealogy in which anti-Petrarchism can have only a very modest share. I do not suggest that the reaction against Petrarchism is of no consequence at all in the development of this kind of anti-feminism in Renaissance poetry; the reaction is there, as the poetry of John Donne clearly attests. Then there is the further possibility that a poet's interest in anti-feminist rebellion as a poetic theme may have driven him to imitate this anti-feminism wherever he found it in Greek and Roman lyric. This possibility, however, only corroborates another point on which I have been insisting, that Renaissance anti-feminism is itself more of a poetic convention than a reaction against the Petrarchan convention; and the widespread occurrence of Petrarchan and "anti-Petrarchan" poems standing next each other in the output of the same poet (Wyatt, Ronsard, Drayton, and Daniel, to mention only four) serves merely to strengthen this view.

I am inclined to think further that a far more sensible and organic anti-Petrarchism is that which manifests itself not as an attack on the poet's lady (which only substitutes one convention for another) but as an attack on Petrarchan poetry as a whole and on the Petrarchan poet himself as an imitator and a fraud. Such animadversions do in fact exist. Probably the most widely known spoof of Petrarchism and its "false compare" is Shakespeare's Sonnet 130; Suckling's almost equally famous "Why so pale and wan" subjects the whole Petrarchan attitude to merciless ridicule; and other instances—in Sidney, for example—can easily be found. Less well known is a brilliant specimen of this anti-Petrarchism (not anti-feminism) by the Juvenalian satirist Joseph Hall, an excerpt from which I cannot forbear quoting:

> The loue-sicke Poet, whose importune prayer
> Repulsed is with resolute dispayre,
> Hopeth to conquer his disdainfull dame,
> With publique plaints of his conceiued flame.
> Then poures he forth in patched *Sonettings*
> His loue, his lust, and loathsome flatterings:
> As tho the staring world hangd on his sleeue,
> When once he smiles, to laugh: and when he sighs, to grieue.
> Careth the world, thou loue, thou liue, or die?
> Careth the world how fayre thy fayre one bee?
> Fond wit-old, that would'st lode thy wit-lesse head

With timely hornes, before thy Bridall bed.
Then can he terme his durtie ill-fac'd bride
Lady and Queene, and virgin deifide:
Be shee all sootie-blacke, or bery-browne,
Shees white as morrows milk, or flaks new blowne.
And tho she be some dunghill drudge at home,
Yet can he her resigne some refuse roome
Amids the well-known stars: or if not there,
Sure will he Saint her in his Calendere.[37]

(Virgidemiæ, I, vii, 6-26)

Here Hall, a critic of some consequence in the late sixteenth century, aims his anti-Petrarchan barbs not at a disdainful mistress, real or imaginary, but primarily at the person who really deserves them, the Petrarchan poet himself. In a number of satires from the *Virgidemiæ* group, Hall vents his exasperation with such poets, who

. . . filch whole Pages at a clap for need
From honest Petrarch, clad in English weed.[38]

(Virgidemiæ, VI, i, 251-252)

This I much prefer to regard as the true anti-Petrarchism. It is an anti-Petrarchism which goes directly to the heart of the matter, and the heart of the matter is not a lady's scorn but the esthetic value of a poem. It is an anti-Petrarchism which lays its censure squarely where it belongs, on the poetry and on the poet, specifically on those sonneteers who doggedly follow the Petrarchan convention while lacking the wit to cloak it with the least semblance of reality or conviction.[39] In this sense, therefore, the libertine cry for vengeance upon a hardhearted lover is not an attack on the Petrarchan convention at all but a poetic convention in its own right. At best it is a mere reversal of Petrarchism, and an accidental one at that, for it clearly occupied a prominent place in amorous poetry many centuries before Petrarch's time. The history of ideas is admittedly complex enough to render the task of denying poetic influence somewhat easier than that of affirming it. Still, oversimplification is no very reliable tool for the literary historian in any of his endeavors; and to allege a revolt against Petrarch as the origin of a poetic theme which was clearly established centuries before Petrarch is to oversimplify a matter which is not quite so easily pinpointed in time. In fact, it is almost a commonplace of human nature (and hence of poetry) that malicious contemplation of his lady's fading charms may well be the last refuge of the disgruntled suitor in any age.

Notes

[1]The article which follows is a considerably expanded version of a paper read at the twenty-eighth annual meeting of the South Atlantic Modern Language Association, held at Augusta, Georgia, November 6-8, 1958.

[2]Cf. Louis B. Salomon, *The Devil Take Her: A Study of the Rebellious Lover in English Poetry* (Philadelphia: University of Pennsylvania Press, 1931), pp. 1-66 *passim*, 259-276 *passim*.

[3]The description is Wyatt's, in the poem beginning "Payne of all payne, the most grevous payne," from the Devonshire MS. Add. 17492. See *Collected Poems of Sir Thomas Wyatt*, ed. Kenneth Muir (London: Routledge and Kegan Paul, Ltd., 1949), p. 129.

[4]*Minor Poets of the Seventeenth Century*, ed. R. G. Howarth (London: J. M. Dent and Sons, Ltd., 1953), p. 67.

[5]See my dissertation (Florida State University, Tallahassee, 1956), "An Analysis of the *Carpe Diem* Theme in Seventeenth-Century English Poetry (1590-1700)" (Ann Arbor: University Microfilms, 1956), Ch. V.

[6]Cf. Ps. 90:5-6, 103-15; Ja. 1:10-11; I Pet. 1:24.

[7]For a detailed account of the significance of Anteros in Greco-Roman myth see Robert Valentine Merrill with Robert J. Clements, *Platonism in French Renaissance Poetry* ("New York University Studies in Romance Languages and Literatures," Vol. I; New York: New York University Press, 1957), Ch. IX, to which I am indebted for much of the information in this paragraph.

[8]*Ibid.*, pp. 183 ff. One such interpretation represented Anteros as the god of spiritual, i.e., neo-Platonic, love, whereas his brother Eros presided over carnal passion. Still another identified him with Lyseros, the dissolver of hopeless love, a function which Renaissance votaries of Petrarchism would doubtless have found extremely useful.

[9]Pausanias, *Description of Greece*, ed. and trans. W.H.S. Jones, 5 vols. ("The Loeb Classical Library"; London: William Heinemann, 1918), I, 165. The italics are those of the translator. Merrill (p. 164) mentions, but does not quote, this account.

[10]The poem, of course, is the well-known "My Lute Awake," in the Egerton MS. 2711. See *Collected Poems*, p. 50.

[11]*The Greek Anthology*, trans. W. R. Paton, 5 vols. ("The Loeb Classical Library"; Cambridge, Mass.: Harvard University Press, 1939), I, 287-288.

[12]James Hutton, *The Greek Anthology in France and in the Latin Writers of the Netherlands to the Year 1800* ("Cornell Studies in Classical Philology," Vol. XXVIII; Ithaca: Cornell University Press, 1946), p. 617.

[13]*Œuvres Complètes*, ed. Gustave Cohen, 2 vols. ([Bibliothèque de la Pléiade," Vols. XLV-XLVI; Paris:] Librairie Gallimard, [c. 1950]), I, 241.

[14]Morris Bishop, *Ronsard: Prince of Poets* (Ann Arbor: University of Michigan Press, 1959), p. 198.

[15]Hutton, p. 373.

[16]Paton, IV, 401.

[17]*Ibid.*, I, 173.

[18]Hutton, p. 600.

[19]*The Love Poems of Joannes Secundus*, trans. F. A. Wright (New York: E. P. Dutton and Co., Inc., 1930), p. 122. Wright translates the passage as follows:

> What profits it with frowns to mar your grace?
> *Too soon will wrinkles spread on that fair face.*
> Nay rather pluck the rose, while yet you may,
> Ere life's bright spring by fate is swept away.

The italics are mine.

[20]Paton, I, 165. Cf. also Marcus Argentarius, *Greek Anthology* v. 118 (Paton, I, 185), cited in fn. 24 *infra*.

[21]Hutton, pp. 596-597.

[22]*Œuvres Complètes*, II, 814. Note that the meter is iambic pentameter, in the English way, rather than the usual Alexandrines of French verse.

[23]*Œuvres Complètes*, II, 63-64.

[24]Here are some others, all taken from Book v of the Anthology, the book devoted to amatory epigrams:

Rufinus, v. 21 (date uncertain; not earlier than the third century B. C.)
Callimachus, v. 23 (third century B. C.)
Rufinus, v. 27 (cf. fn 36 *infra*)
Rufinus, v. 28
Plato, v. 79 (the philosopher)
Rufinus, v. 103
Marcus Argentarius, v. 118 (not later than the reign of Augustus; cf. fn. 20 *supra*)
Macedonius the Consul, v. 233 (sixth century)
Macedonius the Consul, v. 271
Agathias Scholasticus, v. 273 (Byzantine, sixth century)

Still others can be found in Book xii, the *Musa Puerilis* of Strato, an amatory group addressed exclusively to males; cf. fn. 16 *supra*.

[25]The following are a few examples, not including those cited in the text of this discussion:

Vergil *Eclogues* 2. 17-18
Tibullus *Elegies* i. 8. 41-42, 47-48, 77-78.
Propertius *Elegies* iii. 25. 11-18 (a very savage attack)
Martial *Epigrams* vi. 40
Horace *Odes* i. 25; iv. 13

[26]Q. Horatii Flacci, *Opera* (Parma: Bodoni, 1793), p. 154.

[27]C.-A. Sainte-Beuve (ed.) *Œuvres Choisies de Ronsard*, new ed. rev. Louis Moland (Paris: Librairie Garnier Frères, n.d.), p. 133.

[28]*Œuvres Complètes*, I, 505. They are not the concluding lines of Ronsard's poem.

[29]*The Poems and Translations of Thomas Stanley*, ed. Galbraith Miller Crump (Oxford: The Clarendon Press, 1962), pp. 49-50.

[30]*Minor Poets of the Caroline Period*, 3 vols. (Oxford: The Clarendon Press, 1905-21), III, 142.

[31]"Stanley, Sherburne, and Ayres as Translators and Imitators of Italian, Spanish, and French Poets," Part I, *Modern Language Review*, XX (July, 1925), 280-281. (This article was published in two parts, the second of which appears in the October, 1925, issue of *MLR*.)

[32]*Minor Poets of the Caroline Period*, III, 401.

[33]*Anatomy of Melancholy*, Part. 3, Sec. 2, Mem. 5, Subs. 3.

[34]Among the studies which analyze specific classical influences on Herrick may be cited the following: Pauline Aiken, *The Influence of the Latin Elegists on English Lyric Poetry, 1600-1650, with Particular Reference to the Works of Robert Herrick* ("University of Maine Studies," 2d series, No. 22; Orono: The University Press, 1932); and Kathryn A. McEuen, *Classical Influence upon the Tribe of Ben* (Cedar Rapids, Ia: The Torch Press, 1939).

[35]The attribution of this poem to Ayton (or Aytoun) is doubtful.

³⁶For the marked similarity between the Ariosto and Catullus passages cf. Cesare Segre (ed.), *Ludovico Ariosto: Opere Minore* (*"La Letteratura Italiana,"* Vol. XX; Milan: Riccardo Ricciardi Editore, n.d.), p. 846. The notes to the *Orlando Furioso*, which comprises Vol. XIX of the series, are printed in Vol. XX.

The epigram by Philippus is *Greek Anthology* xi. 36 (Paton, IV, 87). That by Rufinus is *Greek Anthology* v. 27 (Paton, I, 143; cf. fn. 24 *supra*).

³⁷*The Collected Poems of Joseph Hall*, ed. A. Davenport (Liverpool: The University Press, 1949), p. 18.

³⁸*Ibid.*, p. 94. Further statements from Bishop Hall on this subject may be found in *Virgidemiæ*, I, i, 5-6; IV, ii, 83-84. Cf. Davenport, Introduction, pp. xxxvi-xxxvii, xlix.

³⁹Hall singles out Daniel and Drayton in particular as highly unoriginal practitioners of Petrarchism. It is significant, moreover, that the attack on the unwilling mistress is almost as striking a convention in these two poets as Petrarchism itself. The *Delia* and *Idea* cycles alone contain many examples.

Part II

ARTIFICE AND ARTISTRY IN *RICHARD II* AND *OTHELLO*

In writing *Richard II*, Shakespeare faced two different problems, one artistic, one political. The artistic problem was how to move into tragedy with materials previously used in *histories*. The impulse to create tragedy must have been strong, for the play is close to the era of the great tragedies, but the effort was only partially successful because *Richard II* is a dramatic hybrid, as Polonius would say, a *tragic-historical*.

The political problem was complex with historical, theoretical, and contemporary complications. Historically, Richard, a legitimate king by inheritance and divine right, was deposed by an able usurper who fathered a great king, who brought the only glory to the nation in a hundred years of bad history. Politically the divine right versus Machiavellian and renaissance ability theories (so ably dramatized by Marlowe in *Tamburlaine*) were dangerously implicit and explicit in Shakespeare's materials, and the late years of Elizabeth's reign afforded no neutral atmosphere for treatment in plays of controversial history and politics.

That Shakespeare surmounted the artistic difficulty at least to a degree is evident from the fact that *Richard II* is good reading and fairly good theatre. That Shakespeare did not go to jail after the play's performance, even after its political use,[1] at least insofar as we know, is indicated by the fact that he solved the inherent political problem to the satisfaction of contemporaries.

How Shakespeare achieved dramaturgical and literary success while avoiding dangerous political implications to risk alienating a part of his audience, even risking arrest, is the subject of this three part study. Section I shows how he injected tragedy into and sustained tragic effects in a history play format. Section II demonstrates how Shakespeare with the use of a technical device presented controversial political materials without risking accusations of personal involvement.

Section III is a transition from *Richard II* into *Othello*.

I

That Shakespeare in writing *Richard II* was on the way from dramatic history to human tragedy has been recognized[2] and can be readily accepted. If Shakespeare intended to forsake histories and make the play into a full tragedy, he had difficulties in spinning out a tragic structure once the tragic character and faults in his Richard were conceived. He allowed the basic tragic fault to operate to a crisis in the middle of the play. His concept seems to have been a Richard who had to sustain his ego with heroic delusions. The concept was so vivid as to be impelling, and Richard's switch from one delusionary world to another comes suddenly and completely, in what is virtually a one-act play in Act III, Scene ii, where Richard turns away from reality and abdicates. This was Richard's tragedy, and the tragic fault is dramatically clear. Shakespeare failed to present Richard in evolution and resorted to (1) poetic declamations mixed with (2) historical episodes to afford "two hours traffic of our stage" for a full play.

From the beginning to Act III *Richard II* had possibilities for being either a history play, with opposing groups contending in episodes to the resolution, or, a tragedy. Richard's public and self-visualized image was established in the opening "audition" scene in which Bolingbroke and Mowbray play their respective "loyal opposition" and "henchman-taking-the-rap" roles.[3] Richard's magnificent-king role was to have no underlying substance (objective correlative), but the position from which he was to fall was established. Political issues and merits of the power struggle were left studiously ambiguous. Dramatic effects were achieved in pageantry of court procedure and the vituperation between aggressive Bolingbroke and defensive Mowbray. As it would have been in reality, basic issues were not allowed to come to the surface where a front was being maintained. The whole court was acting[4] to support the public and assumed role of Richard. The later seemingly superfluous tournament scene is vital in terms of its relationship to Richard's vision of himself as the absolute anointed king of medieval myth.

Aside from a tendency to whimsicality and inclination to dramatize his image of himself, Richard's faults are not obviously and purposefully developed until the dying Gaunt scene. In this scene revelation of flaws in Richard and forwarding of the historical plot are nicely integrated. Vacation of the Lancaster title and the seizure of possessions is a key point in the progress of the main historical plot. Equally important is the exposure of Richard's arrogant bad judgment, the refusal or inability to evaluate elements of reality in the situation. Richard negated the system on which his own position was based. Henceforth, Richard was to have no capacity for adjusting to reality. The compulsion of Richard to live by illusions rather than to adjust to reality was to be the basis of his personal tragedy.

The death of Gaunt scene for another reason was significant in the creative process. Effective use was made of the device of poetic declamation in dying Gaunt's famous eulogy on England, and Shakespeare, for like effects, was to use the device in the latter half of the play to solve the problem of keeping an image of the already tragic Richard before the audience after his real tragedy had been enacted and the plot structure had shifted to that of an episodic history play with Bolingbroke vying for the place of the protagonist.

The final structure of the drama and the hybrid type of play was determined by a schism in the developing action. Richard's real tragedy (mental, with character basis) was staged at the middle of the play, while Bolingbroke's rise to kingship continued through two more acts. After Act III, Scene ii, considerable artifice was necessary to sustain the promise of the first half and to keep the play from falling to the level of a conventional history play.

Richard II presents a move by Shakespeare toward tragedy of character, a type of his tragedy not to appear in his work until *Macbeth*. *Romeo and Juliet* had been a tragedy of Fate at work, with little emphasis on character fault. *Hamlet* was to be a tragedy of situation, and *Julius Caesar* of political and personality complications. *Othello* was to be a tragedy of evil aggressiveness against good, Iago against Othello. It was not until *Macbeth* that Shakespeare accomplished a full length tragedy of character, and many will not concede tragedy in Macbeth because of his obvious criminal guilt and see Macbeth's end only as deserved punishment. *Richard II* must have been, indeed, an experiment in tragedy. As in *Macbeth*, the poetry spoken and dramatic artistry is better than the speaker and the action.

The tragedy of Richard is enacted like a one-act play in Act III, Scene ii. The scene has conventional plot structure with *opening situation, initial incident, steps in rising tension, a false promise of change of direction before the crisis, a crisis* and *climax,* with the results of the tragedy revealed in the denouement speech of the tragic victim.

After the setting of the scene, Aumerle paves the way for the opening exposition of character and situation:

> Yea, my lord. How brooks your Grace the air,
> After your late tossing on the breaking seas?
> (III, ii, 2-3)

Subsequent developments will show that Aumerle's concern was not really with the health of the king but with how he would re-act to what confronted him on his return from Ireland.

The character of Richard with the suggestion of its flaw along with the impending outside tragic force is revealed in Richard's first speech, which after the first statement turns into a soliloquy:

> Needs must I like it well: I weep for joy
> To stand upon my kingdom once again.
> Dear earth, I do salute thee with my hand,
> Though rebels wound thee with their horses hoofs.
> As a long-parted mother with her child
> Plays fondly with her tears and smiles in meeting,
> So, weeping, smiling, greet I thee, my earth,
> And do thee favours with my royal hands.
> Feed not thy sovereign's foe, my gentle earth,
> Nor with thy sweets comfort his ravenous sense;
> But let thy spiders, that suck up thy venom,
> And heavy-gaited toads lie in their way,
> Doing annoyance to the treacherous feet
> Which with usurping steps do trample thee.
> And when they from thy bosom pluck a flower,
> Guard it, I pray thee, with a lurking adder
> Whose double tongue may with a mortal touch
> Throw death upon thy sovereign enemies.
> (III, ii, 4-22)

The histrionics and alliance of self with earth in such a pathetic fallacy must have amazed followers accustomed to supporting Richard's illusions and make-belief postures, for he concludes with:

> Mock not my senseless conjuration, lords.
> This earth shall have a feeling, and these stones

> Prove armed soldiers, ere her native king
> Shall falter under foul rebellion's arms.
>
> (III, ii, 23-26)

It is obvious that Richard's firm convictions are based on mis-conceptions of himself and mis-reading of the situation. The unawareness involves the same kind of dramatic irony found in the opening scenes of *Oedipus Rex*.

Carlisle first tries to engage the king's attention and establish rapport in thought:

> Fear not, my lord; that Power that made you king
> Hath power to keep you king in spite of all.
>
> (III, iii, 27-28)

and then subtly tries to point out to Richard the weakness and impracticality of Richard's assumed position and attitude:

> The means that heavens yield must be embrac'd,
> And not neglected; else [if] heaven would
> And we will not, heaven's offer we refuse,
> The proffer'd means of succor and redress.
>
> (III, ii, 29-32)

Aumerle is less politic in explaining Carlisle's words:

> He means, my lord, that we are too remiss,
> Whilst Bolingbroke, through our security,
> Grows strong and great in substance and in power.
>
> (III, ii, 33-35)

Richard rebukes Aumerle, refuses even to glance at reality. The suggestion of positive action merely serves to prompt Richard to escape further from reality into greater illusion by expanding his self-image to include analogy with the sun and firm alliance with God and the angels, and the irony inherent in the situation is increased with Richard's rising resistance to and the degree of unawareness of reality:

> Discomfortable cousin! know'st thou not
> That when the searching eye of heaven is hid
> Behind the globe, that lights the lower world,
> Then thieves and robbers range abroad unseen
> In murders and in outrage boldly here;
> But when from under this terrestial ball
> He fires the proud tops of the eastern pines
> And darts his light through every guilty hole,
> Then murders, treasons, and detested sins,

> The cloak of night being pluck'd from off their backs,
> Stand bare and naked, trembling at themselves?
> So when this thief, this traitor, Bolingbroke,
> Who all this while hath revell'd in the night
> Whilst we were wand'ring with the antipodes,
> Shall see us rising in our throne, the east,
> His treasons will sit blushing in his face,
> Not able to endure the sight of day,
> But, self-affrighted, tremble at his sin.
> Not all the water in the rough rude sea
> Can wash the balm off from an anointed king;
> The breath of worldly men cannot depose
> The deputy elected by the Lord.
> For every man that Bolingbroke hath press'd
> To lift shrewd steel against our golden crown,
> God for his Richard hath in heavenly pay
> A glorious angel; then, if angels fight,
> Weak men must fall, for Heaven still guards the right.
> (III, ii, 36-62)

Richard has projected himself to the height from which he will fall. The position is one of sheer mental delusions, and Richard will be brought to earth with a series of shocks of revelations, in the manner of Greek classic tragedy.

Salisbury, the first messenger, arrives with the revelation that divine powers are not working for Richard:

> For all the Welshmen, hearing thou wert dead,
> Are gone to Bolingbroke, dispers'd and fled.
> (III, ii, 73-74)

Aumerle points up that the king's reaction is physical as well as mental:

> Comfort, my liege; why looks your Grace so pale?
> (III, ii, 75)

Richard has lost his sustaining self-image of the soliloquy:

> But now the blood of twenty thousand men
> Did triumph in my face, and they are fled;
> And, till so much blood thither come again
>   Have I not reason to look pale and dead?
> (III, ii, 76-79)

Without supporting delusions he momentarily gives up:

> All souls that will be safe fly from my side,
> For time hath set a blot upon my pride.
> (III, ii, 80-81)

Aumerle hastens to recall Richard to a sense of kingship:

>   Comfort, my liege; remember who you are.
>
>   (III, ii, 82)

and Richard struggles to regain self-control:

>   I had forgot myself; am I not king?
>
>   (III, ii, 83)

only to escape into mock heroics in exhorting his cowering self-image:

>   Awake, thou coward majesty! thou sleepst.
>   Is not the king's name twenty thousand names?
>   Arm, arm, my name! a puny subject strikes
>   At thy great glory. Look not to the ground,
>   ou favourites of a king; are we not high?
>   High be our thoughts.
>
>   (III, ii, 84-89)

He returns to the immediate situation enough to grasp at hope from York's forces and to recognize the second messenger. Scroop's greeting presages more bad news, and Richard's imagination, always over-vivid, leaps ahead to anticipate the actual account:

>   Mine ear is open and my heart prepar'd
>   The worst is worldly loss thou canst unfold.
>   Say, is my kingdom lost? Why, 'twas my care;
>   And what loss is it to be rid of care?
>   Strives Bolingbroke to be as great as we?
>   Greater he shall not be; if he serve God,
>   We'll serve Him too and be his fellow so.
>   Revolt our subjects? That we cannot mend;
>   They break their faith to God as well as us.
>   Cry woe, destruction, ruin, decay:
>   The worst is death, and death will have his day.
>
>   (III, ii, 93-103)

Richard receives Scroop's account of the rebellion almost absent-mindedly. He is beginning to find escape from the anguish of having his self-image of magnificent king destroyed and to find increasing satisfaction in a forming peripheral image that will become full-blown for his final escape from reality. Richard is beginning to like a shaping projection of himself as a holy martyr. His mind gropes for possible betrayal by friends, the greatest of treason, and he hits on Wiltshire, Bagot, Bushy, Green:

>   Where is the Earl of Wiltshire? Where is Bagot?
>   What is become of Bushy? Where is Green?

> That they have let the dangerous enemy
> Measure our confines with such peaceful steps?
> If we prevail, their heads shall pay for it.
> I warrant they have made peace with Bolingbroke.
>   (III, ii, 122-127)

Scroop's ironical:

> Peace have they made with him indeed, my lord.
>   (III, ii, 128)

brings a natural rage in Richard that momentarily promises his facing reality:

> O villains, vipers, damn'd without redemption!
> Dogs, easily won to fawn on any man!
> Snakes, in my heart-blood warm'd, that sting my heart?
>   (III, ii, 129-131)

but with the image of suffering his mind leaps ahead to the most famous betrayor of all time and to self analogy with the greatest of martyrs:

> Three Judases, each one thrice worse than Judas!
> Would they make peace? Terrible hell make war
> Upon their spotted souls of this [offense]!
>   (III, ii, 132-134)

Intent upon the new vision of himself, Richard half hears that his Judases have made peace with Bolingbroke by dying, and he is indifferent to Aumerle's inquiry as to the whereabouts of York and his army. Richard's mind has turned from the problem at hand, and he is finding escape in the emotion of self-pity:

> No matter where; of comfort let no man speak.
> Lets talk of graves, of worms, and epitaphs;
> Make dust our paper and with rainy eyes
> Write sorrow on the bosom of the earth.
> Let's choose executors and talk of wills;
> And yet not so; for what can we bequeath
> Save our deposed bodies to the ground?
> Our lands, our lives, and all are Bolingbroke's,
> And nothing can we call our own but death,
> And that small model of the barren earth
> Which serves as paste and cover to our bones.
> For God's sake, let us sit upon the ground
> And tell sad stories of the death of kings:
> How some have been depos'd; some slain in war;
> Some haunted by the ghosts they have depos'd;
> Some poison'd by their wives; some sleeping kill'd;

All murdered: for within the hollow crown
That rounds the mortal temples of a king
Keeps death his court, and there the antic sits,
Scoffing his state and grinning at his pomp,
Allowing him a breath, a little scene,
To monarchize, be fear'd, and kill with looks,
Infusing him with self and vain conceit,
As if this flesh which walls about our life
Were brass impregnable; and humour'd thus
Comes at the last and with a little pin
Bores through his castle wall, and—farewell king!
Cover your heads, and mock not flesh and blood
With solemn reverence. Throw away respect,
Tradition, form, and ceremonious duty;
For you have but mistook me all this while.
I live with bread like you, feel want,
Taste grief, need friends: subjected thus,
How can you say to me I am a king?
(III, ii, 144-177)

That the speech was not and is not to be accepted sympathetically Shakespeare made sure, with the reproving speech of Carlisle:

My lord, wise men ne'er sit and wail their woes,
But presently prevent the ways to wail.
To fear the foe, since fear oppresseth strength,
Gives in your weakness strength unto your foe,
And so your follies fight against yourself.
Fear, and be slain; no worse can come to fight;
And fight and die is death destroying death,
Where fearing dying pays death servile breath.
(III, ii, 178-185)

Carlisle is wrong in thinking Richard fears death, but the speech points up the element of real tragedy. Carlisle, a man who unflinchingly faces up to life and death throughout *Richard II*, cannot understand the real tragedy of Richard the man.

Promised relief from our sense of impending disaster, a standard dramaturgical device used often just before the *crisis* and *climax* in dramatic structures, comes as Richard responds to Carlisle's reproof and seizes on Aumerle's suggestion of possible help from York:

Thou chid'st me well. Proud Bolingbroke, I come
To change blows with thee for our day of doom.
This ague fit of fear is over-blown;
An easy task it is to win our own.
Say, Scroop, where lies our uncle with his power?

> Speak sweetly, man, although thy looks be sour.
> (III, ii, 188-192)

For a moment we have hope that Richard will surmount his character flaws and go into action, but Scroop dashes our hope and wrecks Richard's attempt at readjustment to reality with the last of the piecemeal revelations—York has joined with Bolingbroke, the northern castles have yielded, and all the south is in arms in rebellion.

Richard gives up quickly, over-willingly, for he had ever been incapable of facing facts and taking proper action. He had always acted out illusionary self-images of magnificence. Subjected to a real test of his character when his illusionary world of the magnificent king was shattered, he rejected reality and escaped into a compensating and satisfying self-image of the magnificent martyr. To Richard one type of heroics was as good as another.

How anxious Richard was to retreat into the new role is revealed in his words to Aumerle:

> Thou hast said enough.
> Beshrew thee, cousin, which didst lead me forth
> *Of that sweet way I was in to despair!* (Italics mine)
> What say you now? What comfort have we now?
> By heaven, I'll hate him everlastingly
> That bids me be of comfort any more.
> Go to Flint castle; there I'll pine away;
> A king, woe's slave, shall kingly woe obey.
> That power I have, discharge; and let them go
> To ear the land that hath some hope to grow,
> For I have none. Let no man speak again
> To alter this, for counsel is but vain.
> (III, ii, 204-214)

Richard has literally and mentally abdicated. His tragedy has been enacted in a one-act play, in one scene in the middle of *Richard II*. It must have been, as Travis Bogard has pointed out,[5] that Shakespeare's concept of Richard's real tragedy came upon him too strongly and too suddenly to be denied immediate enactment.

After the one-act tragedy at the center of the play, Shakespeare had no choice but to finish it in the history mode. He faced the problem of keeping a tragic Richard before the audience through two more acts while Bolingbroke waited for circumstances and the vacancy in the governing power to make him king.

Shakespeare solved his problem by having Richard appear in the history scenes intermittently re-enacting his self-image of the great martyr, speaking some of the finest dramatic poems in our language. Richard presented his self-image so vividly and we are so impressed with the poetry that we are tempted to accept Richard's view of himself as martyred and the martyrdom as Shakespeare's interpretation of his historical materials. Why and how Shakespeare escaped indictment for partisan political convictions is worth further exploration.

II

The tragic element in *Richard II* was fully developed by the end of Act III, Scene ii, and the tragic figure was established. The tragic Richard had too much dramatic appeal for the role not to be carried along with Richard's straight part in the remaining history plot. In the remaining action Richard is a static characterization. Whenever he appears he is the same tragic figure of a man escaping from reality and finding compensation in a projected self-image.

Shakespeare sustains tragic effects in the play by having Richard play a part to himself. Other characters, including Bolingbroke, are often puzzled by Richard's histrionics[6] and seemingly nonsense soliloquies as related to the immediate situation. The opposition party had seen and had been a party to Richard's playing the magnificent king but had not witnessed the shattering of that image and the tragedy of its being compensatingly replaced by Richard's self-induced image of the magnificent martyr.[7] This image is not Shakespeare's concept of Richard; it is Richard's projection of himself.

The technical device by which Shakespeare kept the real tragedy before the audience was by the device of play-acting.[8]

Richard is forced by exigencies of the main plot to give some heed to the business at hand, but often his attention is peripheral, for he is engaged with his self-image.

Confronted with Bolingbroke at Flint castle, Richard recognizes the situation but rejects possibilities in Bolingbroke's posture of demanding only redress and chooses to cling to his image of already having been deposed. After lamenting the immediate situation, he retreats into his tragic self-image:

> What must the King do now? Must he submit?
> The King shall do it. Must he be deposed?
> The King shall be contented. Must he lose
> The name of king? O' God's name, let it go.
> I'll give my jewels for a set of beads,

> My gorgeous palace for a hermitage,
> My gay apparel for an almsman's gown,
> My figur'd goblets for a dish of wood.
> My sceptre for a palmer's walking-staff,
> My subjects for a pair of carved saints,
> And my large kingdom for a little grave,
> A little grave, an obscure grave;
> Or I'll be buried in the King's highway,
> Some way of common trade, where subjects' feet
> May hourly trample on their sovereign's head;
> For on my heart they tread now whilst I live,
> And buried once, why not upon my head?
> (III, iii, 143-159)

With half attention to Aumerle's reactions, he continues, to include Aumerle in the vision:

> Aumerle, thou weep'st, my tender-hearted cousin!
> We'll make foul weather with despised tears.
> Our sighs and they shall lodge the summer corn,
> And make a dearth in this revolting land.
> Or shall we play the wantons with our woes
> And make some pretty match with shedding tears?
> As thus, to drop them still upon one place,
> Till they have fretted us a pair of graves
> Within the earth; and, therein laid,—there lies
> Two kinsmen digg'd their graves with weeping eyes.
> (III, iii, 160-169)

Recalled to the immediate situation, Richard comes to earth with an illusionary analogy:

> Down, down I come; like glist'ring Phaethon,
> Wanting the manage of unruly jades.
> (III, iii, 178-179)

When Bolingbroke protests with:

> My gracious lord, I come but for mine own.
> (III, iii, 196)

Richard gives more than is asked, and willingly:

> Your own is yours, and I am yours, and all.
> (III, iii, 197)

> What you will have, I'll give, and willing too;
> For do we must what force will have us do.
> (III, iii, 206-207)

because Richard is anxious to preserve his self-image.

After the Queen-gardener scene, in the parliament scene in which Bolingbroke ably handles the wrangle among the nobles and then at the urging of York ascends the vacant throne, it is necessary for Richard to appear to abdicate publicly. He appears play-acting, in a trance-like state, voicing a recall of the earlier analogy with Christ:

> Alack, why am I sent for to a king
> Before I have shook off the regal thoughts
> Wherewith I reign'd? I hardly yet have learn'd
> To insinuate, flatter, bow, and bend my knee.
> Give sorrow leave a while to tutor me
> To this submission. Yet I well remember
> The favours of these men. Were they not mine?
> Did they not sometime cry, "All hail!" to me?
> So Judas did to Christ; but He, in twelve,
> Found truth in all but one; I, in twelve thousand, none.
>   (IV, i, 162-171)

Reminded of the purpose of the occasion by York and by Bolingbroke of the willing resignation, Richard states truthfully that he will give up the crown willingly but not his self-satisfying tragic role:

> My crown I am; but still my griefs are mine.
> You may my glories and my state depose,
> But not my griefs; still am I king of those.
>   (IV, i, 191-193)

When the impatient, and possibly somewhat confused, Bolingbroke puts a direct question about the resignation, Richard goes into a soliloquy and trance-like play-acting that re-establishes the picture of the tragic Richard when his real tragedy had been enacted at the end of Act III, Scene ii. The speech might well have been a continuation of that Scene, and it serves the purpose of keeping the earlier psychological abdication before the audience:

> Ay, no; no, ay; for I must nothing be;
> Therefore no no, for I resign to thee.
> Now mark me, how I will undo myself.
>
> I give this heavy weight from off my head
> And this unwieldy sceptre from my hand,
> The pride of kingly sway from out my heart.
>   (IV, i, 201-206)

and continues with the image of self-projected martyrdom:

> With mine own tears I wash away my balm,
> With mine own hands I give away my crown,
> With mine own tongue deny my sacred state,
> With mine own breath release all duteous oaths.
> All pomp and majesty I do forswear;
> My manors, rents, revenues I forgo;
> My acts, decrees, and statutes I deny.
> God pardon all oaths that are broke to me!
>
> (IV, i, 207-214)

Complete forgiveness is a part of martyrdom:

> God keep all vows unbroke are made to thee!
> Make me, that nothing have, with nothing griev'd,
> And thou with all pleas'd, that hast all achiev'd!
> Long mayst thou live in Richard's seat to sit,
> And soon lie Richard in an earthly pit!
> God save King Henry, unking'd Richard says,
> And send him many years of sunshine days!
> —What more remains?
>
> (IV, i, 215-222)

Richard cannot face a bill of particulars of his "weav'd-up follies". Therein might be found things to impair his consolation image. The enormity of Northumberland's suggestion throws Richard again into an analogy with the betrayal of Christ (note the re-occurance of this exaggerated image):

> Nay, all of you that stand and look on me
> Whilst that my wretchedness doth bait myself,
> Though some of you with Pilate wash your hands
> Showing an outward pity; yet you Pilates
> Have here deliver'd me to my sour cross,
> And water cannot wash away your sin.
>
> (IV, i, 237-242)

Richard even points up his play-acting with:

> Nay, if I turn mine eyes upon myself,
> I find myself a traitor with the rest;
> For I have given here my soul's consent
> To undeck the pompous body of a king;
> Made glory base, a sovereignty a slave,
> Proud majesty a subject, state a peasant.
>
> (IV, i, 247-252)

Looking upon himself instead of his projected image, Richard comes near the truth but retreats to recall the earlier sun image with Bolingbroke now displacing him as the sun:

> O that I were a mockery king of snow,
> Standing before the sun of Bolingbroke,
> To melt myself away in water-drops!
>
> (IV, i, 260-262)

Richard calls for a mirror to vivify the almost lost martyr image, but looking into the mirror is a shocking disappointment, and he dashes the mirror. Richard's martyr image was a mirage, and a mirror will not reflect a mirage.

Shakespeare used great skill with devices and artistry to keep the real tragedy of Richard before the audience: tragic tone in poetic declamations, re-occuring self-images, effective play-acting—all interwoven into the history plot that demonstrates an able Bolingbroke rising to kingship. On the surface at least, Bolingbroke is virtually entrapped into the kingship by circumstances. The political issues may be suggested, but they certainly are not resolved to the satisfaction of partisan theorists nor to indicate Shakespeare's beliefs and attitudes. Richard is established as a tragic figure but of character not of martyrdom by usurpation.

Interpretations of the play are generally in agreement that Richard finally becomes truly heroic in his death struggle,[9] but for good theatre it scarcely could have been otherwise, and there is some question as to whether this Richard is Shakespeare's Richard or Richard's own most forceful mental projection of himself finally in action. Shakespeare may have reached a point of absorbing his play-acting technique into the main stream of the action of the whole play.

In any case, by following Shakespeare's artistry and artifice, we see, and surely the audience saw, since it would be more apparent on the stage than from reading,[10] that in *Richard II* Richard is martyr only to himself. Shakespeare's attitude toward Richard and the politics involved escapes us because of Shakespeare's artistry in getting dramatic effects without personal involvement. The play is good reading and fair theatre. It affords little knowledge about Shakespeare the man, a great deal about Shakespeare the artist.

III

To go from *Richard II* to *Othello* seems to bridge a long span in Shakespeare's work. The purpose is to go from the seemingly studied art and artifice in *Richard II* to a play which affords finished workmanship.

It is apparent that in writing *Richard II* Shakespeare had a firm sense of tragedy and the value of a central tragic figure, but in that play he did not quite surmount certain dictates of his historical materials and implications of the political issues.

Between *Richard II* and *Othello*, Shakespeare achieved good tragic structures, albeit, in different patterns as if each play were a challenging experiment in a different type of tragedy. Except for inherent strong nationalism, the source materials for *Julius Caesar* were similar in general nature to those of *Richard II*. However, multiple important personages and controversial politics did not impede accomplishment of full evolutionary tragic structure in *Julius Caesar*. Historical events in the play are not so important as history as incidents in the humanized tragedy of individuals, and the politics serve only as surface issues for more basic conflicts of personalities. *Julius Caesar* is human tragedy with a background of history.

The plot pattern of *Hamlet* is different from that of *Richard II* or *Julius Caesar*. In *Hamlet*, the central hero carries forward the action in a struggle against a complex situation existing at the beginning of the play. The part of Hamlet as the protagonist is even different from that of Richard of Gloucester in *Richard III* in that Richard creates sustaining conflict as the plot progresses.

A unified tragic structure in *Hamlet* is achieved in spite of the over-luxurious development of some scenes and the loose episodic aspect of the plot in the script. In working out the stage presentation, Shakespeare must have been influenced by surviving old Hamlet stories and an old play, the mythical *Ur-Hamlet*.

Othello is of quite different design than either *Julius Caesar* or *Hamlet*. In *Othello*, a villainous protagonist starts from a norm and proceeds against a blameless and innocent hero. A single line of rising tragic action, with accompanying irony, results from the efforts of a scheming knave. The issues are individual conflicts, and tragedy stems from deliberate human effort, not from events, situation, or an outside fate.

Shakespeare may have been self-conscious about the loose episodic plot in *Hamlet*, for *Othello* shows extremely tight knitting of the action. To begin with, Shakespeare used a free hand in inventing action and in developing character to suit the needs of the action. Cinthio's story afforded him little more than the suggestion of a plot. Starting with fiction, he was not hampered, as in *Richard II* and *Julius Caesar*, by history and politics.

By the time of the writing of *Othello*, much of the apparent artifice and many of the devices obvious in the earlier plays had become integrated into seemingly effortless method as elements of Shakspeare's natural style. For example, Iago play-acts throughout because putting up a false front has been his natural way of life—"I am not what I am." He plays one part to the audience, another to himself, and another to his fellows on the stage. (Psychological analyzers, as might be expected, have trouble keeping these Iagos apart). The soliloquies, standing out as poetic declamations in *Richard II*, in *Othello* are vital to the action and revelation of underlying irony, irony that often operates in several directions at the same time. Without distortion from applications within the play, extended poetic passages, the truisms of Iago, cannot be as readily extracted for use as from *Richard II*.

The most striking aspect of Shakespeare's artistry is in plot economy and continuity: invention and selection of successive events, economy in depth of scene with omission of everything superfluous to the immediate purpose, puppet-like control of attitudes, acts, movements, and speeches of persons, movement of characters to and from and back to the right spot at the right instant, silence by involved persons about realistically natural phenomena that would detract from the developing complication. Characters keep silent about that which they would naturally speak out (Emilia), and say the right-wrong words (Desdemona) to forward the movement toward disaster. Characters are given the right trait to fit the developing situation (Cassio, Othello, Desdemona).

The key to the plot design in *Othello* lies in the part of Iago. As Iago moves, sometimes intelligently for his own purposes and often, ironically, not so intelligently, so goes the play. The part of Iago, his successive planning with the underlying irony, is the frame upon which Shakespeare built the tragedy of Othello and Desdemona. Abstracted from the matrix of the whole play, the part is something of a variation of a play-within-the-play interspersed with and motivating the developing disaster.

The Tragedie of King Richard the Second, with *new additions of the Parliament Sceane, and the deposing of King Richard.* As it hath been *lately acted* by the Kinges servantes, at the Globe, by William Shake-speare.

From Original Drawing by W. HARVEY

A Deflated Iago

S tudies and interpretations of Iago[11] tend to fall into one of three categories: (1) psychological studies,[12] allegorical interpretations,[13] and (3) dramaturgical analysis.[14] Partisans to the first two categories assume Iago to be a "rounded" static character, either psychologically abnormal or allegorically evil, who from the beginning intended to achieve the catastrophe at the end of the play.

Paul A. Jorgensen has seen Iago in perspective in relation to late Sixteenth and early Seventeenth Century knave literature.[15] Actually Shakespeare needed no more than a knave to construct the action and to achieve a secondary theme in the tragedy.

At the beginning of the play it is apparent that Iago is a knave. The final evil to which he will direct his knavery and the real reasons for his later acts are not made obvious nor are his later acts motivated other than by plot invention. The end and the reasons were progressively determined by Shakespeare's invented action. The dramaturgical quality of the play lies in the artistry in developing the plot, not in conceiving a total character.

Studies of Iago have often gone astray in one of several directions:

(1) assumed that Iago's character was from the beginning equal to the final tragedy achieved, (2) that from the first Iago had in mind a devastating catastrophe for Othello and Desdemona, (3) that a knave needs a motive, (4) that, except, for being caught, Iago had at the end progressed triumphantly in a well designed plan. Not enough attention has been kept centered on the effects of invented action and situation on Iago.

Shakespeare wrote *Othello* not long after *Hamlet,* and there are both negative and positive relationships between the plays. Shakespeare may have been self-consciously aware of the loose plot structure in *Hamlet,* for, not since the careful time structure in *Romeo and Juliet* did he give so much attention to knitting the action as in *Othello.* On the positive side of the relationship is the fact that both Hamlet and Iago adopt plans which are guide-lines for the progressive action in the plays. The two plans are very similar in nature. Both plans involve the establishing of a posture in order to take advantage of chance and expediency in on-the-spur-of-the-moment improvising by the two characters. The device worked well in *Hamlet,* and, with significant reverse variations, it worked well in *Othello.*

Both plans use "playacting". Hamlet "put an antic disposition on" to cover his purpose and actions in catching the King. Iago, a knave, hit on playing "double knavery" in feigned honest concern for his General. Hamlet was motivated by the three commands of the Ghost. Iago's purpose at first was vague even to himself, a desire "to plume up my will in double knavery", involving no more than satisfaction in bolstering his ego by embarrassing and discrediting honest superiors. Hamlet directed and remained in control throughout the implementation of his plan, achieved his foreseen end and executed the King. Iago's plan ironically got out of hand, took its own direction, and, for Iago, came to an unforeseen end for himself. The enslavement of Iago and his entrapment in his own plan afforded a pattern of dramatic irony as a supporting theme in the tragedy. The different ways the two plans are made to work illustrates the possibilities for Oedipian irony in a plot moved forward by means of a protagonist's plan.

Shakespeare made Iago's first move against Othello one of knavery, to create strife and to lay a foundation of distrust. Iago admitted that he had no hope of getting Othello dismissed from the generalship or of breaking up the marriage. Iago's next objectives and the means to the ends are stated immediately after the Brabantio-Senate scene and after some further gulling of Roderigo:

> To get his (Cassio's) place and to plume up my will
> In double knavery — How, how? — Let's see:—

After some time, to abuse Othello's ear
That he is too familiar with his wife.
He hath a person and a smooth dispose
To be suspect, fram'd to make women false.
The Moor is of a free and open nature,
That thinks men honest that but seem to be so,
And will as tenderly be led by th' nose
As asses are.
I have't. It is engend'red.

(I, iii, 399-409)

Up to this time Iago had been merely disgruntled and knavish; now he is villainous, a protagonist with a plan. The plan is general with details to be developed with opportunity and expediency. The plan is knavish, not allegorically evil nor psychologically abnormal for a knave.

Iago's confidence in his plan failed to take into account that Desdemona would not naturally fall into unfaithfulness, as Iago had promised Roderigo, and, although he might lead Othello by the nose, Iago was not allowed to foresee the fury of a disturbed and aroused Othello.

The next move invented for Iago was the verbal assault on the moral integrity of Desdemona on the quay at Cyprus. She was willing to pass the time with light banter, but her mind and heart were away with Othello. Iago sensed that the success of his scheme would need to depend upon manipulations without the aid of the moral downfall of Desdemona. Desdemona's integrity was an inconvenience but no block to his course. He had only to adapt his procedures to work on Cassio and Othello. Iago's mistake was natural to his character, and he is most convincing in adjusting error.

Shakespeare's plotting provided immediate and complete success for the intrigue against Cassio, and the ease of the triumph led Iago into his first major mistake of not stopping with the cashiering of Cassio. Ironically, it had all been too easy. "Double knavery", intrigue with Roderigo against Cassio and deception of Othello had so 'plumed up Iago's will' that in his arrogance Iago enlarged his plan to go on toward wickedness. The move into wickedness was a fatal mistake, one to whirl Fortune's wheel and invite Nemesis into the humanly directed Fate. Even the gods of evil will not be mocked. Realistically, Shakespeare had Iago overestimate himself, underrate others, and misread the total situation. This type of irony had been basic in dramatic art with and since the Greeks. Iago is a knavish Oedipus, with immoral intent.

In the third phase of the Iago action Shakespeare increased the difficulties in the task undertaken and the destructiveness of the objective. The plan was something to tax a Machiavellian master-mind, which Iago was not to have. Iago's shrewdest manipulations were to prove mistakes for him. As usual, Shakespeare completely informed the audience of the coming action, in Iago's arrogant brag:

> . . . for whiles this honest fool
> Plies Desdemona to repair his fortune
> I'll pour this pestilence into his ear
> That she repeals him for her body's lust;
> And by how much she strives to do him good,
> She will undo her credit with the Moor.
> So shall I turn her virtue into pitch,
> And out of her own goodness make the net
> That shall enmesh them all.
>
> (II, iii, 359-368)

In the main, the plan worked, and Shakespeare so subtly developed significant miscarriages in the designs of the villain-protagonist that faults in procedure and miscalculations are scarcely to be perceived except in retrospect.

The aim in the new plan went beyond ordinary knavery, in which Iago had proved himself so able, and extended into wickedness of upsetting minds and destroying personalities. Iago was not intelligent enough nor was his rapport with Evil close enough to carry it all off with impunity. Now, Iago, a poor specimen of a human at the best, was to assume the mystic roles of Irony and Fate. This role the gods, Fortune, and poetic justice would never allow.

Shakespeare, however, worked artistically on the human level with realistic materials. Iago simply would not know Othello as well as he thought he did and would not anticipate Othello's reaction to being "successfully led by the nose".[16]

Shakespeare was busy plotting, not revealing preconceived characterizations. Characterization followed invented action, and after-illusions of real personalities arise or are abstracted from the scenes.

Just as with his earlier schemes, Iago's more ambitious plan was made to work easily and, seemingly well. But there is a difference insofar as Iago's personal situation is concerned. With increasing success in shaping the fate of others, Iago loses control of his plan, is forced to new unforeseen objectives, the accomplishment of which changed his own destiny.

The rapid, but convincing, corruption and breakdown of Othello came about only incidentally because of the character of Iago. Iago did not arrange the time scheme of events nor manipulate the movement of individuals in a stage action that could admit no loose ends. He did not select the key situations. He did not give the right words and acts to Desdemona, Cassio, and Emilia that are so logically essential to credibility in the total development. Iago merely stands in the midst of all this and opportunely does and says the right things for his purposes.

From this point in the play (beginning with Act III), it is Shakespeare's dramaturgy, skill in developing plot, not the character of Iago that makes the drama. Iago is still just a knave but with the added delusion of grandeur of master-minding his own destiny while shaping a destructive fate for others. Reality, real Fate, invented by Shakespeare, was soon to take a hand to force a change in Iago's style of play.

Othello surprised Iago. Shakespeare enlarged Othello's personality to include a new trait necessary to the coming action and to the changing part of knavish Iago. Originally a stable, strong, dignified man in set routines affording set firm beliefs, and then subdued and beaten down by the weight of contrived circumstantial evidence against Desdemona, Othello was given the trait of not being able to endure a state of confusion in uncertainty. He could not live in the area between black and white. Iago should have been warned by:

> I'll see before I doubt; when I doubt, prove;
> And on the proof, there is no more but this,—
> Away at once with love or jealousy!
> (III, iii, 190-193)

but he ironically believed that he could prove by arranged appearances to deceive Othello and that there the matter would rest, but Shakespeare made Othello turn dangerously violent and demand a particular kind of proof:

> Villain, be sure thou prove my love a whore;
> Be sure of it. Give me the ocular proof;
> Or, by the worth of mine eternal soul,
> Thou hadst been better have been born a dog
> Than answer my wak'd wrath!
> (III, iii, 359-363)

Iago is no longer a free agent. Circumstances begin to dictate to Iago. He can, with the aid of Shakespeare's handling of time and inventions of events and speeches outside the scope of Iago's powers as a person, furnish the ocular proof.

Success in furnishing the ocular proof was personal failure for Iago. In the process he could no longer 'plume up his will' in a superman illusion of master-minding his own actions and destiny while manipulating destiny for others. Iago enjoyed devious scheming, but now circumstances dictated his planning and methods. He was clever with suggestion but not good with the direct lie. He disliked personal physical action but was forced more and more to act for himself.

The final objectives of our protagonist were not of his own choosing. He had never spoken of murder. He was not of his own natural volition capable of this ultimate villainy. The chain of events ceased to be of his own forging. Further, convincing ocular proof of Desdemona's guilt brought no point of rest. If Desdemona lived, she would eventually refute the charge of infidelity, and so Desdemona had to die. Shakespeare's Iago was no natural killer, but in panicky desperation he could contrive murders. Roderigo and Cassio might be manipulated to remove each other. The scheme miscarried. Shakespeare's invention, not the designs of Iago, shaped the action to the end of the tragedy. The action does not grow out of Iago's character. Othello had to be made to act quickly before he emerged from a state of emotional and mental derangement. Shakespeare created the mental state, managed the time element, and arranged the assassination scene. Dramaturgy, not psychology, was at work.

By all the rules and principles of dramatic truth and of poetic justice Othello had to die after killing Desdemona.

Insofar as Iago's part in the final Act is concerned, real Fate has taken over from Iago's planned Fate. Forces underway could not save Desdemona and Othello without switching the inventions in the plot to bring about tragi-comedy with a danger of farce, but the forces at work were not now of Iago's design and came not from his natural volition, or, to use a popular modern term, his psychological make-up.

Shakespeare so constructed the remaining action that any loose end or chance event could trip up Iago in the plans he no longer controlled. Shakespeare provided for the revelation of the truth and for the conviction of Iago with the timely appearance of Emilia at Desdemona's death and with one of the most shop-worn devices in Elizabethan drama, the letter left behind, in dead Roderigo's pocket.

Iago's schemes worked as he planned only in the initial stages of the play, when he was a knave with knavish objectives. As a protagonist Iago keeps active throughout the play, but except for the impetus to the action from character in the early stages when his methods and aims were knavish, Iago is the deluded victim of his own efforts to shape destiny. This is irony. It is a subordinate and supporting theme of irony in the larger framework of the irony underlying the major tragedy of Othello and Desdemona. More ironical than the part of Iago is the irony of the fact that Othello and Desdemona were destroyed mentally, morally, philosophically, and physically by a knave who, ironically, destroyed himself when he set out to shape his own and the destiny of others.[17] There is greater irony in the tragedy of Othello and Desdemona. They are more worthy victims of Fate and claim our pity, and, as Shakespeare managed the plot, they could not have done other than what they did.

This analysis of certain phases of *Othello* intended to substantiate two points of view, which may have become somewhat confused as the study went back and forth from one point of view to the other, to say nothing of side glances at interpretations by others. For the sake of clarity, it is perhaps well to state the theses.

From the first it was intended to demonstrate (1) that in retrospective analysis the part of Iago affords a supporting theme of Oedipian Irony in Iago's confident efforts to shape Fate, that his planning and schemes soon got out of control to enmesh him in the total fatalistic destruction, and (2) that the artistic genius of Shakespeare lay in his developing the plot action and situations, not in creating "rounded" psychologically consistent characters. Characterization followed the demands of his plotting in the building of a credible dramatic structure.

The first thesis is related to the second in that the Oedipus-like Iago part was the foundation on which Shakespeare constructed the plot of *Othello*.[18]

IV

Iago was studied first for the reason that his part is the guide-line through the action of the tragedy and lends outline perspective to the structure of the play.

Othello is probably Shakespeare's finest achievement in dramatic art, which is not to say that it is his greatest tragedy. The tragedy is a work of art, not a realistic reproduction of life. There is less life-like ambiguity, less scope and density of human behavior, less luxuriating in the scenes than in most other Shakespearean plays. Economy in selection and development keeps attention centered on what Shakespeare wants taken into the awareness of the audience. Characterization required for the moment, exactly right management of motion and position in the episodes, absolute control of speech at crucial moments to contribute to predetermined purpose—all comprise the artistry that induces an illusion of reality, the purpose and successful achievement of the artistic vehicle.

Shakespeare's artistic purpose rather than effort at naturalistic psychology was the determining factor in his characterizations. All the personalities are plot-ridden to an extent, Cassio and Emilia perhaps most of all.

Cassio, at first, if we read Iago's comments inversely and accept at face value Cassio's appointment to the lieutenancy as competent and deserved, is a tried and trustworthy soldier. A little later (II, iii, 12-28) his unstudied resistance to Iago's insinuations of lechery in connection with Desdemona gives us the impression of a man with wholesome habits of thought with respect to women and sex. At the same time we learn:

> I have very poor and unhappy brains for drinking;
> I could well wish courtesy would invent some
> other custom of entertainment.
>
> (II, iii, 34-37)

"Unhappy brains for drinking" (even two cups would make him drunk) must have been a sudden inspiration on Shakespeare's part, for immediately before (II, i) Shakespeare had given him the necessary fault for the coming action without the susceptibility to alcohol:

> *Iago.* Sir, he's rash and very sudden in choler,
> and haply may strike at you. Provoke him, that
> he may; for even out of that will I cause these
> of Cyprus to mutiny, whose qualification shall
> come into no true taste again but by the displanting
> of Cassio.
>
> (II, i, 278-283)

Iago makes no mention until later of Cassio's being easily intoxicated, only easily provoked to sudden anger, and we must presume that the addition to Iago's plan 'to fix one more cup on Cassio was at the same time an enlargement of Cassio's character and that the brawl before the tavern was a happy added invention. The scene is fetching vaudeville and at the same time lends verisimilitude to a key incident in the plot.

Cashiered, Cassio falls into deepest dejection and ineffectual humility, ready to be led by Iago's suggestion into a somewhat craven course of asking an inexperienced and innocent girl to trade upon her nuptial resources to regain his place.

At the depth of his humiliation, we suddenly find Cassio a gay wencher who keeps a punk (III, iv, 168-201) so that the handkerchief device may be managed and also the eavesdropping scene (IV, i, 49-177) in which Othello thinks Cassio speaks of Desdemona. At this point

Cassio, instead of being sexually lofty-minded, is a simpering reveller in his wenching capabilities (IV, i, 107-177). This is not to besmirch or condemn Cassio; it was all necessary to Shakespeare's artifice in plotting. Finally, Cassio is reverted to the original Cassio to succeed Othello by orders of the Senators of Venice.

From the dropped handkerchief (III, iii, 228) to the death scene (V, ii,). Emilia, unless we assume that she was cooperating with Iago, (which we cannot from the final scene in the play) has very slow associative mental processes not to expose Iago's machinations.

It is difficult to see how:

> My wayward husband hath a hundred times
> Woo'd me to steal it; (The handkerchief)
> (III, iii, 292-293)

were possible when the handkerchief had figured in Iago's planning for so short a time. The vehemence with which Iago took the napkin (III, iii, 300-320) should have fixed it and the incident well enough in her mind for her to associate it with answers to Othello's questions and to think of it as a possible instrument in Othello's rising jealousy. Emilia is not permitted to do much thinking, and she is allowed minimum answers to Othello but never to elaborate or speculate or run on at length, as she does while dressing Desdemona (IV, iii, 26-103), when she is almost as garrulous as the Nurse in *Romeo and Juliet*.

One may wonder what the pre-scene conference (IV, ii) was like in duration and substance before she and Othello enter talking about Desdemona and Cassio (1-19) at the beginning of the famous "Brothel Scene". Or, in the light of the limited time, small world of people involved, the handkerchief incident and allusions to it, Iago's attitude, whom, but Iago, she could have associated with:

> some eternal villain
> Some busy and insinuating rogue,
> Some cogging, cozening slave, to get some office,
> Have not devis'd this slander. I'll be hanged else.
> (IV, ii, 130-133)

Shakespeare seems to have been indulging in a bit of verbal irony while underscoring, for audience suspense, how close Iago was skirting exposure. Lively, quick-witted and sophisticated on occassion, Emilia, when necessary, was made to play the slow-witted "Innocent".

No one in the play is allowed to act or speak other than to contribute to the predetermined line of action. With the characterization of Desdemona, Shakespeare did not need to take many liberties nor to make radical innovations. She is given a common failing in keeping with her basically kind, inexperienced, and responsive nature, but she is used artfully.

Desdemona cannot resist a new wife's temptation to take a hand in and become a part of her important husband's affairs, to be helpful for his own good. Shakespeare makes good dramaturgical use of Desdemona's role of the helpful wife. Ironically, she did not know what she was doing, was playfully over-confident and over-resolute in her promise to help Cassio:

> before Emilia here
> I give thee warrant of thy place. Assure thee,
> If I do vow a friendship, I'll perform it
> To the last article. My lord shall never rest;
> I'll watch him tame, and talk him out of patience;
> His bed shall seem a school, his board a shrift;
> I'll intermingle everything he does
> With Cassio's suit. Therefore be merry, Cassio;
> For thy solicitor shall rather die
> Than give thy cause away.
>
> (III, ii, 19-26)

In her first approach to Othello, she pressed too hard and aroused his impatience (III, iii, 41-82) with her continued insistence on a fixed time for his seeing Cassio:

> (Othello) I will deny thee nothing;
> Whereon, I do beseech thee, grant me this,
> To leave me but a little to myself.
>
> (III, iii, 83-85)

It should be remembered that Iago had just started his campaign of suggestion with "Ha! I like not that" as Cassio and Desdemona had talked, and Cassio had stolen away "guilty-like". A little later, after Iago's quick but efficient work in corrupting Othello's mind, Desdemona is given the mistake of entering and insisting on Cassio's restoration:

> I will not leave him now till Cassio
> Be call'd to him.—How is't with you, my lord?
>
> (III, iv, 33-34)

and she is thrown into confusion by Othello's subtle insinuations, confusion to the extent that she lies about the handkerchief:

It is not lost; but what an if it were?
Oth. How?
Des. I say, it is not lost.

(III, iv, 82-84)

Not only does this lie confirm Othello's suspicions, but Desdemona is given the mistake of returning to the plea for Cassio (III, iv, 93). Ironically, Desdemona returned to the topic of Cassio to divert Othello's attention from the handkerchief. There are no loose ends in this encounter; all is art in dialogue. Desdemona's speeches are not naturalistic but artfully selected; she says exactly the wrong things at the right instant to stimulate Othello's teeming imagination.

Shakespeare never allows Othello, in his progress toward firm conviction of Desdemona's guilt, to miss or forget a poor choice of words or speech which might be misconstrued. First Desdemona uses a wrong word *suitor* and establishes rapport with Cassio:

I have been talking with a suitor here,
A man that languishes in your displeasure.
(III, iii, 42-43)

and, in answer to 'if he went hence now', goes on:

Yes, faith; so humbled
That he hath left part of his grief with me
To suffer with him. Good love, call him back.
(III, iii, 51-54)

It has been pointed out that she was too insistant throughout this scene. Not long after, but after Othello's thorough corruption in the interval that he is demanding "ocular proof", she furnishes circumstantial oral proof in unfortunate choice of words (Shakespeare's choice of words). Responding to Othello's insinuation of over-liberality in the symbolism of her moist hand, she reflects his distorted thought:

You may, indeed, say so;
For 'twas that hand that gave away my heart.
(III, iv, 44-45)

A few lines later she again turns the topic to Cassio's suit, and Othello recalls the incriminating handkerchief, about which Desdemona lied. He misconstrues her:

Then would to [God] that I had never seen 't!
(III, iv, 77)

as is indicated in Othello's:

Ha! Wherefore?

(III, iv, 78)

She uses an ambiguous plural, "Heaven bless *us*" (III, iv, 81), which is taken in the wrong sense by Othello: "Say you?", and she insists, after lying about the handkerchief:

I pray, talk to me of Cassio.

(III, iv, 93)

and goes on:

A man that all his time
Hath founded his good fortunes on your love,

(III, iv, 92-94)

This is too much for Othello, and he leaves the stage. After Othello has been convinced of Desdemona's guilt by the circumstantial "ocular proof" of the handkerchief in Bianca's possession and the arranged eavesdropping, while Othello reads the message brought by Lodovico and listens with half-an-ear to Desdemona's conversation with Lodovico, she makes an unfortunate slip of the tongue in referring to the division between Othello and Cassio:

A most unhappy one. I would do much
T' atone them, for the love I bear to Cassio.

(IV, i, 243-244)

The speech incites Othello's "Fire and brimstone.", and he strikes her in rage after she innocently remarks about Othello's being ordered home with Cassio left in command:

Trust me, I am glad on't.

(IV, i, 249)

In the subsequent "Brothel Scene" Othello turns away from Desdemona's one direct question:

To whom, my lord? With whom? How am I false?

(IV, ii, 40)

with "Ah, Desdemona! Away! away! away!", because he believes her persistent in falsity, and after his two raving speeches, she is given another damaging line:

Alas, what ignorant sin have I committeed?

(IV, ii, 70)

Desdemona is now done with the helpful wife role, for it has served its purpose, but in the death scene her words can be and are misconstrued:

> Then Heaven
> Have mercy on me.
>
> (V, ii, 33-34)

and

> O, Heaven, have mercy on me!
>
> (V, ii, 57)

are taken as confession and repentance, for Othello responds, "I say, amen". He discounts the next speech because he thinks she persists in lying about the handkerchief:

> And have you mercy too! I never did
> Offend you in my life; never lov'd Cassio
> But with such general warranty of heaven
> As I might love; I never gave him token.
>
> (V, ii, 59-61)

Her "O! my fear interprets. What, is he dead?" (V, ii, 73) and "Alas, he is betray'd and I am undone" (V, ii, 76) can be and are taken by Othello as final surrender and full confession.

With the right-wrong words Desdemona is made to help convict herself. In *Othello* layers of irony are heaped upon the underlying irony of the total action, and it all is a matter of artistry, not psychology or moralistic philosophy, just ironic fatalism, and that is what makes the tragedy so terrible.

Instances of Othello's character being bent to necessities of the plot have been pointed out in tracing the Iago part. Other examples may be cited: the tendency to abstraction where Iago starts his process of suggestion (III, iii, 35-ff.), fixed ideas and mental sets from recalled words and misinterpreted incidents (from III, iii on), uncontrollable imagination (III, iii, 335-357) and (IV, i, 35-42), trauma from emotional stress (IV, i, 43), cynical play-acting in the "Brothel Scene", and rationalized self justification in the role of executioner for the "cause" at the beginning of the death scene; then he is reverted to an enraged killer in the actual smothering of Desdemona.

Like the others, Othello is not a rounded psychological character, but a plot-ridden human figure. His psychology is true only at the particular incident in the plot, and the action progresses with such speed, managed movement in the episodes, and singleness of concentration that all through the action and at the end an illusion of reality is achieved.

Attention to Shakespeare's artifice and artistry in Othello tends to fix limits for substantive interpretations, if we adhere to Shakespeare's work without escaping into induced illusion of our own making. Of course, Shakespeare's aim must have been to produce a vehicle that would transport our imaginations into an illusion of reality, but we ought always be aware of whether, while interpreting *Othello*, we are analysing Shakespeare's work or our own imaginary *Othello* world.

Notes

¹At the time of the Essex uprising, with the hope of Essex supporters to arouse the London populace.
All references in this study to the text are to the New Cambridge Edition, *The Complete Plays and Poems of William Shakespeare*, edited by W. A. Neilson and C. J. Hill, Houghton Mifflin, 1942.

²Travis Bogard, "Shakespeare's Second Richard," PMLA, LXX, No. 1, March, 1955, pp. 192-209.

³See John Palmer, *Political Characters of Shakespeare*, London, 1945, pp. 188-138.

⁴Leonard F. Dean, "*Richard II:* The State and the Image of the Theater," *PMLA*, LXII, 1952, pp. 211-218.

⁵See the concluding sentence of Bogard's article, *op. cit.*, p. 209.

⁶Note the reactions of his companions throughout Act III, Scene ii, Northumberland's description of Richard as speaking " . . . fondly, like a frantic man" in the scene before Flint Castle, Bolingbroke's attempts to humor and sooth him (including ordering the mirror), and Northumberland's impatient interruptions of Richard in the parliament-abdication scene.

⁷Karl F. Thompson, with references to J. D. Wilson, Hardin Craig, E. K. Chambers, H. B. Charlton, G. B. Harrison, and Marc Parrott in text and footnotes, summarizes various views as to Shakespeare's reflected concept of Richard as a hero and analyses Richard as a martyr in the light of (1) Christian martyrdom and (2) martyrdom in Foxe's *Book of Martyrs, Shakespeare Quarterly*, VIII, No. 2, 1957, pp. 159-166.
Mr. Thompson seems to assume that Shakespeare saw Richard as martyred by the action in the historical plot, with all the political and partisan implications.

⁸Shakespeare had extensively and effectively used the play-acting device in *Richard III.* Richard of Gloucester acts a part to the audience, a part in the action, and a part to the other characters in the play. Richard of Bordeaux in the throes of escape compulsion acts a part to himself. Shakespeare has Gloucester play-act insincerely with diabolical intent. Richard II believed in his own projected image, indifferent to companions and opponents. Shakespeare made use of the device in different ways for different artistic purposes in many of his plays.

⁹See Thompson, *op. cit.*, p. 161.

¹⁰The reader may get entrapped in the poetic passages. It is common in Shakespeare's plays to find the poetry better than the speakers or the situation: witness Richard III, Richard II, Iago, Edmund, Lear, and, especially, Macbeth. The reader becomes taken with the poetry to the detriment of the total action in the play. This

was Shakespeare's way of getting reactions in the audience, reactions unwarranted by realistic analysis of the situation.

[11]Marvin Rosenberg makes references to significant Iago literature in "Defense of Iago," *Shakespeare Quarterly*, VI, pp. 145-158, and in *The Masks of Othello*, University of California Press, 1961, pp. 286-301.

All references in this study to the text are to The New Cambridge Edition, *The Complete Plays and Poems of William Shakespeare*, edited by W. A. Neilson and C. J. Hill, Houghton Mifflin, 1942.

[12]Leo Kirschbaum, "The Modern Othello," *ELH*, XI, pp. 283-296; Brents Sterling, "Psychology in Othello," *Shakespeare Association Bulletin*, XIX, pp. 135-144; Richard Flatter, *The Moor of Venice*, William Heinmann, LTD., London, 1950.

[13]Harold Goddard, *The Meaning of Shakespeare*, University of Chicago Press, 1951; Paul Siegel, *Shakespearean Tragedy and the Elizabethan Compromise*, New York, 1957; Terence Hawks, "Iago's Use of Reason," *Studies in Philology*, LVIII, pp. 160-169.

[14]E. E. Stoll, "An Othello All-too Modern," *ELH*, XIII, pp. 46-57, and *Art and Artifice in Shakespeare*, New York, 1933; Moody E. Prior, "Character in relation to Action in *Othello*," *Modern Philology*, XLIV, pp. 225-237.

[15]"Honesty in Othello," *Studies in Philology*, XLVII, pp. 557-567.

[16]In the coming section of the play, Shakespeare had to enlarge upon the characterizations of Desdemona and Othello by giving them traits, traits quite surprising in the light of the earlier part of the play, to justify the new action and situations. The thesis of progressively creating character to justify progressing action is a study outside the scope of this article.

[17]The play has been so effective that there is always the temptation to put the imagination to work in search for vitalities not explicit in the text. At one time or another most of us succomb to Shakespeare's ambiguity. One of my teachers insisted that the love between Othello and Desdemona was not destroyed, but I do not know where it went after the play ended. Nor do I know whether Desdemona was saved and Othello damned in a Christian frame of reference. (See Paul N. Siegel, "The Damnation of Othello," *PMLA*, LXVIII, p. 1069, and Edward Hubler's comments on the Christian view of the play: "The Damnation of Othello: Some Limitations on the Christian View of the Play," *Shakespeare Quarterly*, IX, p. 295.) I also fail to see any constructive philosophical implications in the play with reference to any known system of moral philosophy other than possibly reverse application to the *Analects* of Confucius or conformity with Greek Fatalism and its attendant sense of Irony.

The Shakespeare method of progressive invention and development of action with characters acting as they must in the situations has posed a problem to directors and actors tied to the concept that basic character is central to a play, with character determining the action. For difficulties in presenting a "rounded" consistent Othello see Marvin Rosenberg, *The Masks of Othello*, University of California Press, 1961. From Rosenberg's analysis of historic productions and Actor's efforts, it is apparent that even the greatest of actors have had trouble with psychological conceptions of character and philosophical interpretations of the play. To overcome this difficulty with actors, a director might claim the privileges of an athletic coach and send in substitutes to meet the demands of particular scenes. The action could go forward effectively without the drag of efforts at psyhcological consistency. Scholars and critics have had as much trouble as the actors with psychological analysis, forgetting that there is no more of the character than is in the play at the moment, except as we enlarge on Shakespeare's work with our own imaginations.

The absence of philosophical consolation in the play is what makes it so fearfully tragic.

[18]Since gradually outgrowing a predilection for psychology in literature, acquired during my graduate study days, I have been puzzled by the general reluctance to accord artistry in plotting a significant place in creative activitiy. Perhaps it is because plots in summary seem so inane, and we can find no "objective correlative" for plots in real life. Correlative points with reality are to be found in the particulars with which plots are developed. Shakespeare has only to make us believe at the moment, and his plots are a succession of such moments.

DUQUESNE UNIVERSITY LIBRARY   870.8   6422

John I. McCollum, Jr.

Part III

WILLIAM HARRISON: A SIXTEENTH-CENTURY MIND

William Harrison's contribution to English social history has long been recognized and highly celebrated. Indeed it is generally conceded that our knowledge of Elizabethan middle-class life would be considerably diminished had not Wolfe and Holinshed enticed the good rector of Radwinter to dash off what he with jocular modesty called his "foule frizeled Treatise." Harrison was close to the prominent historians of the day—in addition to Wolfe and Holinshed and their immediate associates, he knew well Sir Thomas Smith, William Camden, and John Stow—to name only a few of the better known. His own *Chronologie*, which was never published, was expected to be an important contribution to English letters. In the "crums" of that work which he "scambled vp" as the *Description of Britaine and England* he granted to us a delightful view of many aspects of sixteenth-century England. Even more important, he incidentally revealed the perspectives, the personal attitudes and reactions of an intelligent, outspoken (often candidly and naively blunt) Englishman of the rising and increasingly important middle-class. We have then not only a description but, equally useful, the unaffected and perhaps unintentional revelation of how a man of that class might react to what was going on about him. The inclusions and omissions may be significant. Moreover, it is of some importance to view the somewhat spontaneous or casual work

53

of a recognized historian in the light of the critical attitude that governed the work of his predecessors and contemporaries.

Harrison lamented in the original (1577) edition that the suddenness of the request to prepare a manuscript, the shortness of time allowed in the writing, and the speed in the printing made it difficult to use fully the materials which otherwise might have been available. However, he informs us through his prefatory statement to Lord Cobham that he made use of a variety of sources: his "memorie" of much reading in English and classical antiquities (undertaken "toward the furniture of a Chronologie"), such helps as his friends could purchase (though not specifically identified), Leland's commentaries (though "vtterlie mangled, defaced with wet and weather, . . . vnperfect through want of sundrie volumes), "letters and pamphlets, from sundrie places & shires of England," and his conferences "with diuers, either at the table or secretlie alone." Moreover, he "had some repaire" to his own library some forty miles distant, "but not so great as the dignitie of the matter required, and yet far greater than the Printers hast would suffer," and last, the report of "old men yet dwelling in the village where I remaine." Apparently he had been promised other assistance which was not forthcoming. He refers, for example, to the necessity of abbreviating his description of the islands and rivers of the country because of his own lack of knowledge and the failure of friends to deliver information promised (I, xi, 45; I, xvi, 107).[1]

The product was an uneven affair—at times digressively and bookishly pedantic, at others to the point, informative and, always, however, full of himself. In some instances, writing of matters concerning which, by his own admission, he knew nothing, he is trivial and gossipy; yet even when he is stuffing his pages, he enlivens the matter with personal comment or reflection or by an outburst of moral condemnation or patriotic approval. In general, the book is rich in the assurance of candidly personal observation and experience—even if that experience is nothing more than a reaction to his reading or his attitude concerning a momentary problem brought to his mind by what he was writing. So casual is his handling (or so hasty was his writing) that he gave little regard to the "choice of stile, or words" or method, "thinking it sufficient, trulie and plainelie to set foorth such things as I minded to intreat of, rather than with vaine affectation of eloquence to paint out a rotten sepulchre...." What he "minded to intreat of" reveals much about the concerns of an intellectually vigorous parson of the Elizabethan age, whose attitudes quite possibly are those of the greater part of the social group of which he was a member.

Like most of the historians and chroniclers of the time, he leaned heavily, and often uncritically, upon his predecessors. Like them also, he perpetuates misconceptions, legends (instead of history), errors, and superstitions. Much of what passed for history in the sixteenth century was in fact little more than a re-statement of preceding attempts to chronicle the affairs of mankind from the moment of creation to the writer's present. Typically Harrison began his *Description of Britaine* with an account of the division of the earth after creation, a relation of the legendary history of the British isles, and a chapter devoted to the possible existence of giants in pre-historic Britain. His catalogue of kings begins with Samothes, includes Albion, Brute, Locrine, and ends with Elizabeth. Holinshed's *Chronicle*, though more ambitiously conceived and broader in scope than many others, is generally thought to be characteristic of the type; the list of authors "from whome this Historie of England is collected" contains 180 names besides a note of "diuers other bookes and treatises of historicall matter . . . the names of the authors being vtterlie vnknowne." For the compendious *Chronicle* Holinshed wrote or compiled a history of England, using familiar material from traditional sources; Harrison in lieu of an original treatise simply translated Hector Boece's earlier work to provide a *Description of Scotland* ("onlie with the losse of three or four daies"); with similar impunity Holinshed pieced together a *History of Scotland* from Boece, "interlaced sometimes with other authors." John Hooker provided a chronicle of Ireland by merely translating Giraldus Cambrensis; Harrison's *Description of England*, although heavily derivative, is without doubt the most original section.

Many such histories were compiled as an open attempt to celebrate what the authors saw as the achievement and destiny of the nation. They generally included traditional and mythological as well as historical elements to support national claims of divine guidance and favor. As a common feature they included an account of prehistoric Britain, the origin of the people, the coming of Brute and some note of his descendants. Rarely was new material introduced until the author began to record near contemporary events.

A common theme for sixteenth-century histories was, quite naturally, the establishment of the Tudors and the union of the houses of Lancaster and York with the marriage and accession to the throne of Henry VII and the succession of Henry VIII. The horrors of a divided monarchy, the joys of union, the legitimacy of the Tudors were usually points of major interest. Into this treatment was merged the Tudor claim of descent from the British Arthur and of fulfillment of the prophecies regarding the restoration of British kings to the throne, announced in part by Henry's marching to claim the throne under a banner displaying the Red Dragon of Cadwalader.

To the nationalistic and patriotic themes was added a moral element, if not dominant certainly strong. Many writers and their readers saw in the records of the past God's judgments delivered on the unchanging nature of human character. Sir Philip Sidney stated as a convention in his *Defence of Poesy* that the purpose of history was to teach virtue by bidding the reader to "follow the footing of them that have gone before." The pages of history were repositories of *exempla* useful for advising both the magistrate and the commonwealth. Although Harrison's purpose is simply to give a description of his country, his frequent moral interpolations and digressions would not to his contemporaries seem out of place.

For most of the writers of histories after the twelfth century, Geoffrey of Monmouth (frequently supplemented by reference to Nennius, Gildas, and Bede, whom Geoffrey had used) was the chief source. His prominence in Tudor England was even more greatly enhanced by the popular appeal of the Arthurian material for which he was a major source. Although Geoffrey's authority had frequently been debated prior to the sixteenth century, a more questioningly critical attitude was evidenced in the work of Robert Fabyan, for whom many of the older legends were merely "ryght mysty storyes, doughtfull and vnclere," and Polydore Vergil, who rejected as fabulous many earlier accounts of the exploits of such figures as Brute, Brennus, and Arthur and wrote an *English* rather than a *British* history. Out of the debate over the authenticity of the Galfridian Arthur developed a sixteenth century "battle of the books,"[2] owing in part to the contemporary appeal of the Arthurian story to the Tudor monarchs, who traced not only their legitimacy and the justness of their imperial aspirations through Welsh tradition to the legendary king but British claims for religious independence from Rome on the grounds of antique separation. Although Polydore's position was doomed in Tudor England, he did bring a refreshingly analytical attitude and a disposition to a more critical use of sources to English historiography. Later writers like More, Halle, Grafton, Camden, and Bacon asserted as a commonplace that the principal object of the historian was not necessarily the discovery of lessons of virtue or the justification of previously held convictions but the reporting of facts, their causes and effects, from contemporary evidence when possible.

William Harrison was to some extent a transitional figure mixing credulity with judgment, a harsh rationality with a romantic antiquarianism. There is no direct evidence that he was particularly concerned with the historiographical debate, but on a number of occasions he refers pointedly to his close friendship with Sir Thomas Smith, his indebtedness to John Leland, who had led the attack on Polydore Vergil's position regarding English antiquities, and his respect for John Caius, who had argued for an Arthurian patronage of Cambridge. Harrison's position is usually careful and judiciously tentative. His main guide, he tells us, is simply "an especiall eye vnto the truth of things." He suggests, for example, that the works of such writers as Gildas, Polydore Vergil, and Humphrey Lloid might be "corrupted" or in error regarding the topography of Britain. In recounting the legend of St. Albans (II, xiii, 191-2), he rejects an account of the loss of an historical record, "sauing . . . a few notes . . . concerning the death of their Albane," with a brusque marginal comment, "This soundeth like a lie." Relating the order of knighthood, he takes among his contemporaries a moderate position which accepted the historicity of Arthur but subjected reports of his deeds to critical scrutiny:

> I might at this present make a long tractation of the round table and estate of the knights thereof, erected sometimes by Arthur the great monarch, of this Iland; and therevnto intreat of the number of his knights, and ceremonies belonging to the order, but I thinke in so dooing that I should rather set downe the latter inuentions of other men, than a true description of such ancient actions as were performed in deed. I could furthermore with more facilitie describe the roialtie of Charles the great & his twelue peeres, with their solemne rites and vsages; but vnto this also I haue no great deuotion, considering the truth hereof is now so stained with errours and fables inserted into the same by the lewd religious sort, that except a man should professe to lie with them for companie, there is little sound knowledge to be gathered hereof worthie the remembrance. (II, v, 159; see also I, xxii, 120)

In a similar critical vein while dealing with the partition of England into shires and counties, he refuses to conjecture concerning the division of land before the time of Alfred, fearing to lead "peraduenture the reader from the more probable, intangle his mind in the end with such as are of lesse value, and things nothing so likelie to be true, as those which other men haue remembred and set downe before me. . ." (II, vi, 153; see also II, xiii, 190).

Further critical discernment is to be noted when he repeats as "absurd reports" stories relating to the reputation of various springs and waters of the world:

> Manie other such like toies I could set downe of other welles and waters of our countrie. But whie should I write that for other men to read, whereto I giue no credit my selfe . . . sith I take them but for fables, & far vnworthie that anie good man

> should staine his paper with such friuolous matters as are re-
> ported of them, being deuised at the first by Satanas the father
> of lies, for the holding of the ignorant & credulous in their
> superstitions and errors. (II, xxi, 211)

But amusingly enough, despite his protestations, he could not resist stain-
ing his own paper a bit by the re-telling of a few of the stories. In fact,
Harrison is very much the story teller, and herein lies much of his charm.
His reader discovers that he must have attended the old men of the
villages he visited as carefully as he did his books. Despite his professed
inclination to reject the truthfulness of many of the tales and superstitions
he ran across in his researches, he cannot forgo the pleasure of repeating
them.

> It would seeme a wonder [he interrupts his description of fish
> 'taken vpon our coasts' to tell us]; and yet it is beleeued with
> no lesse assurance of some, than that an horse haire laid in a
> pale full of the like water will in short time stirre and become a
> liuing creature. But sith the certeintie of these things is rather
> prooued by few than the certeintie of them knowne vnto
> manie, I let it passe at this time. (III, iii, 224)

He reports naively the interbreeding of a mastiff and a male tiger in India
and notes gravely that in "Archadia . . . copulation is oft seene betweene
lions and bitches" (III, vii, 232). Then with charming frankness and
resignation to the truth of things he writes of other wonders closer to
his home:

> If I should say that ganders grow also to be gelded, I suppose
> that some will laugh me to scorne, neither haue I tasted at
> anie time of such a foule so serued, yet haue I heard it more
> than once to be vsed in the countrie, where their geese are
> driuen to the field like heards of cattell by a gooseheard, a
> toie also no lesse to be maruelled at than the other. For as it
> is rare to heare of a gelded gander, so is it strange to me to
> see or heare of geese to be led to the field like sheepe: yet so
> it is. . . . (III, ii, 223)

Although he records the efficacy of some baths and hot wells in healing
"palsie, dimnesse of sight, dulnesse of hearing, but especiallie the collike
and the stone, old sores and greene wounds," he is generally inclined to
caution,

> . . . sith rumors are now spred almost of euerie spring, & vaine
> tales flie about in maner of euerie water, I surcease to speake
> at all of anie other, till experience doo trie whether they be
> medicinable or not. (II, xxiii, 215)

Despite such care for the truth of things, Harrison at times can be exceptionally credulous and uncritical. For example, he apparently does not question the historicity of Brute, Samothes, Albion, and other quasi-mythological figures (I, vii; II, ix); he makes use of the legendary accounts of the founding of cities, knightly orders, and the institution of laws. His respect for Leland is such that he repeats tales and popular myths solely on his authority. Often when he makes note of the report of others, he appends an expression of his own disbelief or reservation of judgment regarding the truth of the matter; as frequently, however, he does little more than accept the opinions and reports of others, often through many hands, as his own.

Much of his natural history he garnered from classical sources as well as from the reports of his contemporaries and from his own observations. Philostratus, Pliny, Strabo, Livy, Virgil, Sallust, Apollodorus, Aristotle, and Caesar are among those most frequently represented. Among the early historians he refers to Caesar, Tacitus, Nennius, Gildas, Bede, and Hector Boece (Boethius), to mention only a few. Of the English chroniclers, his most frequent references are to Henry Huntingdon, William of Malmesbury, Matthew Paris ("and others before him"), and more vaguely to "common historiographers," to "our writers," to "our old and ancient histories," and to the witness of "old records." His favorite contemporary sources are John Leland, John Bale, Cardan, Sir Thomas Smith, Stow, and Camden. He seems to have had access to much manuscript material. Henry Huntingdon's *Chronicle,* which he quotes in English, though written in the twelfth century, was not published until 1596, by Sir Henry Savile. Similarly, Leland's *Commentaries* ("latelie come to my hands") was not published until 1709; in addition, he seems to have had access to information from Camden, Stow, and Ortelius, who had not yet published. Harrison further referred to his use of charts and maps belonging to "Maister Sackford," to "diuerse records, charters, and donations (made in times past vnto sundrie religious houses)," and to old books in his personal possession. The product is a rich mixture of scholarly investigation, uncritical compilation, gossip, and wondering comment.

Like many other writers of the latter part of the century, Harrison reveals a vast love for his own country and a decided distaste for things not English, particularly when the foreign influence was tinged with Roman Catholicism. Much of the generally unfavorable reaction to Polydore Vergil's work may be attributed to the fact that he was of Italian origin and a Catholic attacking attitudes and traditions which lay at the heart of sixteenth-century English patriotism. Not infrequently does Harrison lament contemporary attraction to things not English: "But such alas is our nature, that not our own but other mens do most of all delite vs . . ." (III, ix, 235). His pride in England is hardly bounded. English carpenters, artisans, merchants, husbandmen, and their products he finds to be justly admired throughout the world. English builders and architects "are in maner comparable in skill with old *Vitruuius, Leo Baptista*, and *Serlo*" (II, xii, 188). With similar pride he reports the variety of food, the wealth of tables, the number and worth of serving dishes, the splendor and style of fashionable dress and the adornment of the persons of the nobility and commoner alike. He luxuriates in the greatness of English inns, the glory of her cities, churches, and universities. Indeed, he asserts, the world serves England.

Although he described with obvious pleasure the almost limitless extent of English wealth, his ingrained moralism would not let him escape the scourge of a nagging conscience. "Oh [he laments] how much cost is bestowed now adaies vpon our bodies and how little vpon our soules!" (II, vii, 172) Of the excesses in dress and fashionable affectations he wryly commented, "Some lustie courtiers also and gentlemen of courage, doo weare either rings of gold, stones, or pearle, in their eares, whereby they imagine the workemanship of God not to be a little amended" (II, vii, 172). But regardless of the excesses and the mishandling of prosperity, Harrison sees all as evidence of God's special approval of his country. "God be praised therefore, and giue vs grace to imploie it well. . . . Neither doo I speake this in reproch of anie man, God is my iudge, but to shew that I do reioise rather, to see how God hath blessed vs with his good gifts" (II, xii, 188). England was a land of free men, Harrison points out, "by the especiall grace of God and bountie of our princes" (II, v, 163). And her natural resources bespeak further his bounty:

> With how great benefits this Iland of ours hath beene indued from the beginning, I hope there is no godlie man but will readilie confesse, and yeeld vnto the Lord God his due honour for the same. For we are blessed euerie waie, & there is no temporall commoditie necessarie to be had or craued by anie nation at Gods hand, that he hath not in most aboundant maner bestowed vpon vs Englishmen. . . . (III, x, 236)

There are in spite of great accomplishment many aspects of English society which Harrison could hardly find the grace to approve. His middle-class background, his protestantism, his modest economic status, perhaps his rural habitation—all are reflected in his reaction to contemporary English life. Of the professions, the law is most roundly condemned; the wealth of the land flows into the pockets of lawyers. ("They wax rich apace, and will be richer if their clients become not the more wiser and warie hereafter" II, ix, 180). Poor men and their difficulties with the law tempt him to digress from his historical treatment of English law, but he satisfies himself with the hope (though pessimistically held) that lawyers might apply themselves with more conscience to the service of the needy (II, ix, 181). Despite their rapacity, he agrees that they could hardly succeed were it not for the "nature of our countriemen, that as manie laws are made, so they will keepe none; or if they be vrged to make answer, they will rather seeke some crooked construction of them to the increase of their priuat gaine. . ." (II, xxii, 213).

Even his admired merchants, tradesmen, and artificers are criticized for becoming too quickly anxious for and accustomed to luxury, for their sacrifice of honorable industry and pride in workmanship in order to gain additional wealth. His survey of the nation's resources is punctuated by frequent angry condemnations of encroachment and the monopolistic practices of landlords and middlemen. As a poor man himself and as a university man, he deplores the corrupt devices by which the children of poor men are defrauded of scholarships and shut out of English schools, their places usurped by the rich who bribe officials (II, iii, 149). A poor minister ("for what great thing is forty pounds a year"), he regrets the impositions made upon his income in the form of taxes, appeals, and visitations and defends the practice of pluralism as providing a worthy man means for a living and the church means of securing a worthy minister (II, i).

And characteristic of spokesmen for all ages, he fears the loss of the nation's strength in the disappearance of her natural resources and in the growing materialism and social follies of his contemporaries. Surveying the nation's forests, for example, he is constrained to reflect on the changing nature of national strength:

> In times past men were contented to dwell in houses, builded of sallow, willow, plumtree, hardbeame, and elme, so that the vse of oke was in maner dedicated wholie vnto churches, religious houses, princes palaces, noblemens lodgings, & nauigation: but now all these are reiected, and nothing but oke anie whit regarded. And yet see the change, for when our houses were builded of willow, then had we oken men; but now that our houses are come to be made of oke, our men are not onlie become willow, but a great manie through Persian delicacie crept in among vs altogither of straw, which is a sore alteration. (II, xxii, 212)

Like many an Englishman caught in the surging nationalism of Elizabeth's reign, Harrison pointedly condemned the current predilection for Italian fashions and manners. As to Ascham, the Italianate English-man was to Harrison the very devil incarnate. He saw, with so many others, the Italian fashion to be reprehended on religious and moral as well as on patriotic and social grounds. He repeats most of the clichés in his criticism. The Italian danger was so insidious, he warned, that the country would soon be ruined if the evil were not reformed; both "noblemens & meane gentlemens sonnes . . . bring home nothing but meere atheisme, infidelitie, vicious conuersation, & ambitious and proud be-hauiour, wherby it commeth to passe that they returne far worsse men than they went out" (II, v, 162). Even his admiration for the great English universities is tempered somewhat by his disapproval of the professors who sojourn in Italy "from whense verie few without speciall grace doo returne good men" (II, iii, 150). But happily he can announce with his middle-class pride that English artificers and husbandmen can be "merie without malice, and plaine without inward Italian or French craft and subtil-tie . . ." (II, vi, 168).

His distrust of foreigners is no less than his hatred of the Roman Catholic church and is justified on essentially the same grounds. His fre-quent comparison of the ecclesiastical practices of his present with the Roman Catholic past portrays a clergy negligent of its calling and a corrupt hierarchy inclining more to foreign than to English interests, consumed by personal and public ambition, greed, and proud ungodliness. In true Protestant fashion, he attributes papal opposition to the "translation of the seruice of the church into the vulgar toong" to fear that such practice "might breed the ouerthrow (as it would in deed) of all his religion and hierarchie . . ." (II, i, 138). Although he finds reason for rejoicing in the reduction of "our holie and festiuall daies," he would remove them all from the calendar "as neither necessarie nor commendable in a reformed church" (II, i, 138).

His desire for and delight in the reformation of the physical ap-pearance of the churches, he tempers with a bit of practical frugality:

> As for our churches themselues, belles, and times of morning and euening praier remaine as in times past, sauing that all images, shrines, tabernacles, roodlofts, and monuments of idolatrie are remooued, taken downe, and defaced; onlie the stories in glasse windowes excepted, which for want of sufficient store of new stuffe, and by reason of extreame charge that should grow by the alteration of the same into white panes throughout the realme, are not altogither abolished in most places at once, but by little and little suffered to decaie, that white glasse may be prouided and set vp in their roomes. . . .
> (II, i, 138)

Similar approval of plainness and decorum is to be noted in his reference
to the garb of the reformed clergy, now "more decent than euer it was
in the popish church," when "to meet a priest . . . was to behold a pea-
cocke that spreadeth his taile when he danceth before the henne: which
now (I saie) is well reformed" (II, i, 139). References to the papal nobility
are uniformly disparaging (and often amusingly so). Dunstan is "the
author of all their pride and presumption here in England," he reports.
Thomas à Becket is "the old cocke of Canturburie" imitated by the "yoong
cockerels of other sees" (II, i, 133).

His most vigorous condemnation stated a popular national bias;
Roman Catholicism, he argued, has perverted the loyalty of Englishmen
from proper service of their princes. This appeal to the national and
monarchical interest is repeatedly expressed in his recitation of the past
history of the church as well as in his analysis of the sixteenth-century
protestant achievement. Under the sway of the Roman church, he wrote,
the prelates, following Becket's lead, "protested that they owght nothing
to the kings of this land, but their counsell onelie, reseruing all obedience
vnto the see of Rome. . . . Kings were to rule no further than it pleased
the pope to like of; neither to chalenge more obedience of their subiects
than stood also with their good will and pleasure" (II, i, 133-4). With
what approbation might his monarch note Harrison digressing characteristically from his *Description* to ask his readers,

> Is it not strange, that a peeuish order of religion (deuised by
> man) should breake the expresse law of God, who commandeth
> all men to honour and obeie their kings and princes, in whome
> some part of the power of God is manifest and laid open vnto
> vs? (II, i, 134)

And it is no wonder, he reflects in a rich metaphoric vein, that the
pope chafes at the loss of England; financially ". . . our Iland was one of
the best paire of bellowes . . . that blue the fire in his kitchen, wherewith
to make his pot seeth" (II, ii, 146). Contemporary payments to the
crown of England, he judges, are hardly to be compared with the "store
of coine . . . transported out of the land vnto the papall vses" (II, ii, 146).
A married clergyman himself and having defended the marriages of protestant priests and ministers earlier in the *Description*, Harrison could
hardly be expected to resist a jibe at the Roman assumption of a celibate
priesthood. Referring to the pope's provision of the see of Canterbury
for Egidius, a nephew of Sylvester, he notes parenthetically, "for nephues
might say in those daies; Father shall I call you vncle? And vncles also;
Son I must call thee nephue" (II, ii, 142). Nor could he restrain a derog-

atory reference to "times past" when ecclesiastical livings were "furnished with strangers, especiallie out of Italie," who had little skill in "discharging of those functions wherevnto they were called by virtue of these stipends" (II, i, 135).

From such characteristic evidence it may be observed then that in his handling of church history as in his description of contemporary ecclesiastical conditions, Harrison, as might be expected, reveals a thoroughgoing English nationalism and a closely puritanical protestantism. In this he is most certainly a man of his age and class. It is worth noting, as well, that his churchmanship is essentially that of a pastor, not a theologian, involving moral conduct and church polity rather than the more intricate doctrinal debates. Typical of his concern is the following comment:

> I would wish that I might liue no longer than to see foure things in this land reformed, that is: the want of discipline in the church: the couetous dealing of most of our merchants in the preferment of the commodities of other countries, and hinderance of their owne: the holding of faires and markets vpon the sundaie be abolished and referred to the wednesdaies: and that euerie man, in whatsoeuer part of the champaine soile enioieth fortie acres of land, and vpwards, after that rate, either by free deed, copie hold, or fee farme, might plant one acre of wood, or sowe the same with oke mast, hazell, beech, and sufficient prouision be made that it may be cherished and kept. (II, xxii, 213)

Reviewing the sum of the *Description*, one notes from his omissions as well as his inclusions that his interests are broadly rural and middle-class, somewhat puritanical at times. There is, for example, very little said of the actual management of governmental matters or of foreign relations; nor is there much of the court, except what he might gather by hearsay. These matters, as he states candidly in reference to the Queen's palaces, are beyond his knowledge, "sith my calling is and hath beene such, as that I haue scarselie presumed to peepe in at hir gates . . ." (II, xv, 195); or in military matters, "What hath the long blacke gowne to doo with glistering armour? what sound acquaintance can there be betwixt Mars and the Muses? or how should a man write anie thing to the purpose of that wherewith he is nothing acquainted?" (II, xvi, 199)

Similarly, there is but a passing reference to what must have been one of the most exciting aspects of the English achievement—the privateering and the voyages of discovery and colonization: "I might take occasion," he wrote, "to tell of the notable and difficult voiages made into strange countries by Englishmen, and of their dailie successe there: but as these things are nothing incident to my purpose, so I surcease to speake of them" (II, xvii, 201). One wonders perforce what direction of purpose led him to discuss instead the state of the navy in Saxon and Norman times or to compare the modern English naval armament with that of the Roman and Carthaginian. How rich might have been a description in his rare colloquial style of the London shipping district into which such a variety of people and goods flowed from both the old and new worlds. What we get instead is perhaps a reflection of his preoccupation with the effects of commerce with foreign countries on English husbandmen and tradesmen. We have his comment on the disadvantages Englishmen suffer in exchanging their goods on the world market and, of course, an account of the national wealth that allows Englishmen to buy such items as Venice glass, foreign wines, foods and spices from Spain, Portugal, the Indies, and the Americas. These, however, when Harrison sees them are already in English pantries and on the tables far from the noise and excitement of the quays, ships, and traders.

Harrison was apparently well read in the historical literature of England and seemed to have some respect for Chaucer, Gower, Lydgate, Fox, and Jewell; there is no mention, regrettably, of his literary contemporaries. Even a negative comment, which might well be expected, would be attractive. By the time of the first edition (1577) and certainly by the printing of the second (1587), a notable body of poets and story tellers had appeared. Because he was close to some of the literary activity and apparently familiar with the printing houses (he possibly had been brought to London to work with Holinshed at the suggestion of a relative, John Harrison, a London printer), what a loss it is that we do not have something from his hand concerning this now active craft. Although he made mention of vagabonds, beggars, and thieves, he ignores the sonneteers, the anthologizers, the hack writers, the advice books (surely approving the purpose of the *Mirror for Magistrates*), or the moral treatises and allegories. Similarly, considering his sense of judgment and balance in other matters, we lament his failure to note in passing, at least, the Italian influence on English letters; although it is probable that such literature would be thought little more than the "vaine toies" of frivolous minds. There is nothing of the public amusements although the Theatre had been completed in 1576 and the Curtain and Blackfriars opened in 1577. The obvious fact is that Harrison's interests did not lead him in the direction of aesthetic pleasures. His delight in the luxuriousness of the great houses, the architectural skill of their design, the creativeness of the English artisans, the variety and splendor of dress and ornament, the number and expanse of English rivers, or the fecundity of English gardens and orchards reflects not an appreciation of their beauty but pride in English possessions and respect for English success in economic matters, even though he might, on occasion, bewail the dangers of that success to the moral fiber of the nation.

Although he devotes the principal portions of Books I and III and approximately one-fourth of Book II to descriptions of the topography and natural resources of the countryside, he gives us very little of the life and manners of rural folk, a subject with which, as a country parson, he must have been quite familiar. If what we have in Book II is the description of London promised in Book I (xi, 47), he provides very little in the nature of a description of the city or its multifarious activity. What we have seems to be the somewhat casual or superficial observation of surface activity rather than an analysis of civic life. His interests are principally antiquarian, religiously reformed and somewhat materialistically middle-class. His personal knowledge of English life in its broader aspects is limited; indeed, he reminded Lord Cobham that "vntil now of late" he "neuer trauelled 40. miles foorthright and at one iourney" in all his life. In honesty, he repeatedly reminded his reader that he reported little from firsthand, and he is discovered stuffing his chapters with material, not always to the point, drawn from ancient writers, with gossip, absurd tales, and personal digressions intermixed. He seems to be most enthusiastically devoted to rural and agrarian matters (gardens, orchards, woods, country fairs and markets, livestock, and wild life), frequently commenting on the economic implications of the situation under discussion. He familiarly reports on limited aspects of life among the urban middle-class, but seems to be most at home in English antiquities; indeed, few chapters, regardless of the subject, fail to include antiquarian matter.

What is of inestimable value here is the mind that brings us not only what he sees (or chooses to discuss) in Tudor England but a vigorous reaction to what interests or concerns him. His greatest contribution may well appear not so much in the actual description which is the subject of his book (though that is valuable) but in the digressions in which he reflects, rebukes, laments, rejoices, or praises much of what was commonplace to most of his contemporaries. Fortunately, the view is that of a learned, intelligent, and vocal man, full of life, strong opinions, and deep love for his country, who, while intending to describe his country, unwittingly revealed a charming portrait of a man very possibly representative in his interests and attitudes of an increasingly large and important class of Englishmen, a class that within a hundred years would control the destiny of the nation.

Notes

[1]Citations of Harrison's text are noted parenthetically and refer to the 1587 (second) edition of Holinshed's *Chronicle* for which the *Description of Britaine and England* was revised. To make possible reference to other editions of Harrison's works more easily accessible, the citations include identification of book and chapter as well as pagination of the sixteenth-century text.

[2]See Edwin Greenlaw, *Studies in Spenser's Historical Allegory*, Baltimore, 1932; Charles Bowie Millican, *Spenser and the Table Round*, Cambridge, Mass., 1932; and Josephine Waters Bennett, *The Evolution of "The Faerie Queene,"* Chicago, 1942.

Part IV

TWO FACES OF STYLE IN RENAISSANCE PROSE FICTION

The sixteenth century was a time of experiment in the forming of English prose style, a time when writers like Elyot and Ascham thought they were producing useful books, not contributions to literature. The need for written communication in a society that was becoming increasingly literate and democratic was so strong that learning to write effectively in prose was imperative. The main stream of English literature, revived by the change in spirit of the age, was to find expression in poetry and drama; but how to write satisfactory English prose was relatively unknown. Some of the many haphazard experiments were imitative and some fantastic; in fact, the Renaissance period was one of trial and error, an age in which the novel as a distinct genre did not yet exist.[1] Several examples, however, of what may more properly be called prose fiction, written in various manners about diverse kinds of people, were created. Since these became popular with a large number of readers, they naturally took on different forms and appealed to different kinds of audiences.

Commentators about the English novel have had a general tendency to find some kind of "development" in the prose fiction of the Renaissance. Wilbur L. Cross, for instance, uses for his book on the novel the title *The Development of the English Novel*, and of the medieval verse tales he affirms that "Fiction is expanding and taking a step toward the freedom of the modern novel"; in his *History of the English Novel*, Ernest A. Baker diligently attempts to trace the "development" of Elizabethan prose fiction; Richard Church, in turn, traces "the art of story-telling" and claims a place of importance for the contributions of the Renaissance; Edward Wagenknecht finds that Lyly's work "seems curiously prophetic" of what would be written later, but C. S. Lewis recognizes a general "advance from medieval art" to which Lyly's *Euphues* fails to contribute; and, finally, Lionel Stevenson believes that to some extent Nashe's *The Unfortunate Traueler* "can be classified as the first historical novel" produced in England, thereby making an attempt to demonstrate a kind of development.[2]

Yet the Renaissance in England is notable for two faces of style used in prose fiction which seemingly are of greater importance than the concept of the development of the novel. These two manners of writing, with some overlapping, of course, can be readily recognized: first, *estilo culto*, an artificial mode of expression traced back to Gorgias, the ancient Greek orator, which is best represented by the euphuism of John Lyly and the arcadianism of Philip Sidney; and, second, the native, more realistic prose tradition existing in England from medieval times, that was practiced occasionally with some degree of success by such writers as Robert Greene, Thomas Nashe, and Thomas Deloney.

I

One of the best known producers of prose romance of the time was John Lyly, a clever young man and a product of the universities, who strongly desired the court appointment of master of the revels. One may suspect that his main purpose in writing *Euphues, or The Anatomy of Wit* (1578) was to display his brilliance. His professed purpose, as he stated it in his dedication, was, nevertheless, to study human nature and to provide models for the improvement of manners and morals:

> . . . in all perfect workes aswell the fault as the face is to be showen. The fairest Leopard is sette downe with his spots, the swetest Rose with his prickles, the finest Veluet with his bracke. Seing then that in euery counterfaite as well the blemish as the bewtie is coloured: I hope I shal not incur the displeasure of the wise, in that in the discourse of Euphues I haue aswel touched the vanities of his loue, as the vertues of his lyfe. . . . For as euery Paynter that shadoweth a man in all parts, giueth euery peece his iust proporcion, so he that disciphereth the qualities of the mynde, ought aswell to shew

euery humor in his kinde, as the other doth euery part in his colour.[3]

The plot of *Euphues* is a simple triangle in which two friends who fall in love with the same girl have their problem finally solved when she marries another man. But the plot is a mere pretense for the author to make moral reflections in the form of long letters and conversations on such subjects as friendship, love, education, conduct, and religion, with an expression of disapproval of immoralities like atheism, drunkenness, and sexual excesses. The characters are only sketchily developed, existing primarily to enunciate Lyly's ideas; and the setting is equally vague. With the folly of love as the principal idea, Lyly published in 1580 a second part of this work, *Euphues and his England.* His continuation of the tale, though, is largely a repudiation of the harangues against women and love between the sexes contained in the first part. Here Lyly made a special appeal to English ladies as well as to the men, because by this time he had realized that several of his readers were women.

Lyly's prose romance was notably successful, but the author soon turned to writing plays instead of fiction. No doubt some of the recognition of his highly elaborate prose work came from turning to profitable account the "courtesy books" which had originated in Italy and become popular in England because the English were taking the Continental ideal of a gentleman as their own model. Although what is now called "euphuism" had existed for some time before Lyly adopted it,[4] *Euphues* was the best known popular example in England of this special use of language.

Euphuism as it is generally known consists of two elements: the complicated and somewhat poetic rhetoric known as *estilo culto* and the use of similes taken from ancient learning and mythology, from the so-called "unnatural history" which aroused the derision of writers like Sidney, Nashe, and Harvey. Especially conspicuous were the similes descended from the fictitious natural science of medieval bestiaries and well-known encyclopaedias of knowledge that were popular before the invention of printing. For ages, indeed ever since the time of Gorgias, orators and preachers had used such illustrations, just as trained writers had loved to employ the *schemata.*

The poetic elegance of euphuism was based on figures of sound, not sense. It depended largely on the *schemata,* or word-schemes. Isocolon, meaning equality of limbs, is a balancing of phrases or clauses by means of their close matching in length or weight. Thus the symmetry of euphuism—sometimes believed to be monotonous—was created. Parison, meaning equality of sound, is the echo of word to word in such examples as "suspect me of idleness" and "convince me of lightness." In these clauses, which are of about the same length, the contrasted words appear at the same places in their structure. Paromoion, meaning similarity of sound, includes alliteration, the close repetition of consonants, generally at the beginnings of words; assonance, the close repetition of terminal sounds; and the repetition of syllables within the words. Lyly used various forms of paromoion to intensify the other correspondences. His most obvious device is alliteration, with the added variation of transverse alliteration (e.g., "Let thy tune be merry when thy heart is melancholy"). Such syllabic antitheses also as the echoing of "lightness" and "lewdness," and "hopeless" and "hapless," and the rhyming of unstressed syllables, as in "nature" and "nurture," achieve like effects. This balancing of elements which have similar sound schemes gives the sentence a symmetrical structure somewhat like that of verse. Clauses may be formed into opposing pairs that are like couplets, and by means of still more complicated correlations a sentence may be developed almost into the form of a stanza of verse. Sentence may be joined to sentence so closely that an entire paragraph consists of cadences which take on an interlacing unity. Although antithesis is the most notable characteristic of euphuism, it is important to note that it was used not so much for the sake of the meaning as for the pleasure given by approximate but contrasted sounds. The principal aim of this kind of writing, then, was to impose a symmetrical form upon language and thereby to impress upon prose effects equivalent to metre and rhyme.[5]

An example of Lyly's achievement, short but typical, is found in the section called "A cooling Carde for Philautus and all fond louers":

> If thou bee so nice that thou canst no waye brooke the practise of Phisicke, or so vnwise that thou wilt not beate they braynes about the institutes of the lawe, conferre all thy study all thy time, all thy treasure to the attayning of the sacred and sincere knowledge of diuinitie, by this maist thou bridle thine incontinencie, raine thine affections, restrayne thy lust. Heere shalt thou beholde as it were in a glasse, that all the glorye of man is as the grasse, that all thinges vnder heauen are but vaine, that our lyfe is but a shadowe, a warfare, a pilgrimage, a vapor, a bubble, a blast, of such shortnesse that *Dauid* sayth it is but a spanne long, of such sharpnesse, that *Iob* noteth it replenished with all miseries, of suche Vncertaintie, that we are no sooner borne, but wee are subiecte to death, the one foote no sooner on the grounde, but the other ready to slippe into the graue.[6]

Critics disagree in their opinions about Lyly's contributions to Eng-

lish prose. Ernest A. Baker, on the one hand, contends that Lyly made
a beneficial advance in his use of rhetoric and that his sentences were
real sentences, not "paragraphs clumsily knit into lengths of meandering
discourse that came to a halt when nothing more could be hitched on."[7]
C. S. Lewis, on the other hand, declares that he "cannot agree with critics
who hold that *Euphues* marks any advance in the art of fiction"; and he
furthermore places Lyly among the "drab and transitional" writers of the
sixteenth century rather than in the "Golden" period simply because he
wrote *Euphues*, "that fatal success."[8]   It seems obvious that these two
perceptive critics did not consider the concept of two faces of Renaissance
style, one of which was well illustrated by Lyly's popular composition.

The success of *Euphues* was all its young author desired. Before the
publication of the second part, four editions of the first had been printed;
and Lyly's production was extensively imitated, both in content and manner, for about a dozen years. Then it gradually faded into oblivion, to
be superseded by another representative of *estilo culto*, the arcadianism
of Philip Sidney.

Between 1577 and 1580 Sidney wrote for his sister, the Countess
of Pembroke, a prose romance, *The Countess of Pembroke's Arcadia*,
which he called an "idle worke." Although Sidney at this time was young
and not yet knighted, he had gone on foreign embassies and been admired by some of the prominent authors of the time. He did not, in
fact, desire publication. He thought, rather, of his story as being so
frivolous that it would impair his reputation as a serious poet and critic.
In a letter which accompanied part of the manuscript sent to his sister,
he wrote in a derogatory manner of his book, but in a mode typical of
his employment of English prose:

> Here now have you (most deare, and most worthy to be
> most deare Lady) this idle worke of mine: which I fear (like
> the Spiders webbe) will be thought fitter to be swept away,
> then worn to any other purpose. For my part, in very trueth
> (as the cruell fathers among the Greekes, were woont to doo
> to the babes they would not foster) I could well find in my
> harte, to cast out in some desert of forgetfulnes this child,
> which I am loath to father. But you desired me to doo it, and
> your desire, to my hart is an absolute commandement. Now,
> it is done onelie for you, onely to you: if you keepe it to your
> selfe, or to such friendes, who will weigh errors in the balaunce
> of good will, I hope, for the fathers sake, it will be pardoned,
> perchance made much of, though in it selfe it have deformities.
> For indeede, for severer eyes it is not, being but a trifle, and
> that triflinglie handled.[9]

The *Arcadia* was not published until 1590, four years after the author's death. The printed version is unlike the surviving manuscripts, and the book known by most of its readers is the one published in 1593 as a composite text. Sidney apparently realized after the completion of his romance that it was more than the "trifle" he had thought it to be.

The first *Arcadia* was a complex tale, but it was narrated in a straightforward manner. In the second version, the reader is plunged at once into the middle of complications which attempt to conform to epic conventions of the time. Frequently the main characters relate preceding events to their friends and thus maintain the element of suspense by means of interruptions. Sidney's courtly readers must have found enjoyment in tracing the many threads of the plot and in finding that they all eventually brought an orderly conclusion.

The importance of the *Arcadia* does not lie primarily, however, in the plot; the young author's dreamy poetical language casts a spell upon the reader. Again, like Lyly, Sidney created an unusual method of writing. Consisting largely of descriptions, details, metaphors, similes, and conceits, "its essence," as C. S. Lewis has noted, "is fullness, its danger, overfullness."[10] Most of the sentences are long; whether or not they are too long may be a debatable matter. Although the arrangement of the elements of the sentence, peculiar to Sidney, is not perfect, it is appropriate in many ways to the anthropocentric attitude of the Elizabethans toward nature.[11] And Sidney's manner of expression seems suitable for the imaginary land of Arcadia which is the setting of his plot. One sentence from a descriptive set piece illustrates the hazy atmosphere, in which the author includes many general details but few exact descriptions:

> There were hilles which garnished their proud heights with stately trees: hūble valleis, whose base estate semed cõforted with refreshing of silver rivers: medows, enameld with al sorts of ey-pleasing floures: thickets, which being lined with most pleasãt shade, were witnessed so to by the chereful depositiõ of many wel-tuned birds: each pasture stored with sheep feeding with sober security, while the prety lãbs with bleting oratory craved the dams cõfort: here a shepheards boy piping, as though he should never be old: there a yong shepherdesse knitting, and withall singing, & it seemed that her voice cõforted her hands to work, & her hãds kept time to her voices musick.[12]

Sidney's prose fiction, like Lyly's, required an appropriate style. Sidney, however, disliked Lyly's work, as he noted in his *Defence of Poesie* where, in the later sections, he wrote about the contrived nature of much of the verse and prose of his age. But like Lyly, he too attempted to create

II

a work of art by realizing beauty in the workmanship as well as in all other facets of his tale. He thought of all creative literature as poetry; thus the *Arcadia* in prose he considered almost as a poem, with imagery, diction, and rhythm expressing the harmony necessary for the ideality and exalted feeling of the narrative. In his *Defence of Poesie* he asserted that "the greatest part of Poets have apparelled their poeticall inventions, in that numbrous kind of writing which is called *vers*. Indeed but apparelled verse: being but an ornament and no cause to Poetrie."[13] Thus for Sidney the word *poesie* could include prose fiction. Only metre was lacking; his creation therefore contained sufficient ornamentation to make it poetical. But unlike Lyly, he needed an unrestrained and flowing language in which he could arouse the reader's delight in sensuous description. Yet, Sidney was unable to achieve his ideal, for, whereas he disliked effusive imagery and tiresome likenesses, he composed many incongruous tropes and conceits. And if he attempted to avoid "similiter cadences," he tended to overtemper his narrative and dialogue with a surfeit of sweetness. His arcadianism is, then, very different from Lyly's euphuism; but they were two popular kinds of *estilo culto*, each of which was no doubt the result of a true understanding of the nature of style without the ability to use it perfectly. Since Sidney demonstrated that in all likelihood he did not care for Lyly's work, the conclusion may be drawn that he attempted something different because of influence by reaction, a counter tendency to the qualities which he disapproved of in Lyly's *Euphues*.

Readers found delight in Sidney's *Arcadia* long after *Euphues* had been practically forgotten. By 1600 four editions had been printed, and in the seventeenth century fourteen more were issued. One reason for the great popularity of this "idle worke" probably is that the author's extravagant embellishments seem to become less noticeable as one reads through the book and that there is more reality in it than the reader at first suspects.

Lyly and Sidney wrote no more prose fiction, but they were followed by numerous imitators who flagrantly took advantage of the opportunity provided by *Euphues* and the *Arcadia*. Anthony Munday published, for instance, in the same year as the second part of *Euphues*, his *Zelauto: The Fountain of Fame*, "given for a friendly entertainment to Euphues at his late arrival into England"—an obvious imitation; and Barnaby Rich deliberately followed the plot of *Euphues and his England* in the Second Tome of the *Travels of Don Simonides* (1584). John Day, Beaumont and Fletcher, and Shakespeare certainly, also used fragments from the *Arcadia*.

In the second face of Renaissance style in prose fiction, a certain amount of realism appeared, descending presumably from sources entirely different from those of *estilo culto:* in part from the jest-books and somewhat from an interchange between historians and producers of fictitious literature, but mainly from the older native tradition of English prose. There is no doubt that the jest-books were ancestors of the more realistic fiction, but they contributed nothing toward connected narrative. The historians of the time employed facts as often as they could; then they added touches of character and bits of dialogue to enliven their scenes. At the same time, composers of imaginary tales attempted to win readers by using some of the devices of historians and biographers or other kinds of reporters. This interchange developed a reciprocal influence between the two efforts to provide reading material and thereby gave new life to factual accounts and lent an air of credibility to fanciful stories. Such a circumstance, naturally enough, led to the popularity of quasi-journalistic prose. Then gradually many feigned pieces of writing, often no more than pamphlets, assumed the guise of real occurrences. Although some of these attempts were largely "borrowed" from other authors, the final result was a decisive advance in narrative skill.

On the whole, writers of *estilo culto* followed a general trend of the time when the word *artificial* was one of praise; but the confusion of genres and influence by reaction turned some creators of invented tales toward common life as subject matter for their productions. Their less spectacular mode of expression, instead of being patterned after classical models or being dreamily remote from ordinary life, consisted mainly of the simple colloquial or collective sentence, with sprawling units having no conscious parallelism of structure or poetical language, but connected loosely by temporal and co-ordinating conjunctions. It was also readily expanded by the use of cataloguing, by the piling up of synonyms, and by the inclusion of words with corresponding meanings or of phrases having similar construction. When oral ornament was desired, it added alliteration and synonymous pairs of words. The over-all effect was unemphatic.[14] Instead of the formal pattern constructed by Lyly, for example, shapelessness was the general characteristic of this prose. It was essentially a polysyndetic and adequately co-ordinated language through which, in a more carefully controlled form, was transmitted, through Tyndale, the native tradition of English prose in the English Bible.

The fiction written in this ostensibly realistic and somewhat journalistic manner appealed not so much to the courtly audiences of Lyly and Sidney as to the common people. Deloney's productions especially seem to have been written for a class that has often been thought unable to read. But it is most likely that reading in Renaissance England was more prevalent than has usually been considered. The grammar schools gave thorough training in language, and it is believed that they "cultivated the ground from which flowered the great vernacular literatures" of the time.[15] The reading public included many members of the middle class, such as merchants and shopkeepers. And also, women read, not only ladies at the court, but "house maids and harlots" as well.[16]

Typical of the confusion of genres and the experiments being made in the new forms of reading material were the exposures of social evils, in which writers called attention to the criminals and outcasts who infested London, to the ill-doings of moneylenders, to the tricky devices of greedy tradesmen, and to the nefarious deceptions practiced by unscrupulous lawyers. Readers were interested in life as they saw it or imagined it to be.

Since the unplanned, cumulative sentence was suitable for describing ordinary life or that of the lower classes, Robert Greene found it advantageous in his popular works, which may be considered an approach to sociological realism. After he had turned out about twenty little tales in an attempt to emulate Lyly's formula, he won greater recognition with his more realistic accounts of the evils of London. His first cony-catching pamphlet, *A Notable Discouery of Coosnage, Now daily practised by sundry lewd persons, called Connie-catchers, and Crossebiters*, went through three editions in 1591. Appropriately dedicated to "the young gentlemen, merchants, apprentices, farmers, and plain countrymen," it warned them about the tricks of card-sharpers and swindlers with women. Greene's representation of the fleeced "cony," written in sentences that are simple and aggregative, is both vivid and moving:

> Then the barnacle's card comes forth, and strikes such a cold humour unto his heart that he sits as a man in a trance, not knowing what to do, and sighing while his heart is ready to break, thinking on the money that he hath lost. Perhaps the man is very simple and patient, and, whatsoever he thinks, for fear goes his way quiet with his loss (while the cony-catchers laugh and divide the spoil), and being out of the doors, poor man, goes to his lodging with a heavy heart, pensive and sorrowful, but too late, for perhaps his state did depend on that money, and so he, his wife, his children and his family, are brought to extreme misery.[17]

The Second and last part of Conny-catching, published about the same time, exposes five other kinds of deceit; and *The Thirde and Last Part of Conny-Catching*, published in 1592, consists of ten picaresque tales, supposedly written from notes given to the author by an elderly justice of the peace. Among Greene's other pamphlets there is one, *The Conversion of an English Courtesan,* which adumbrates the theme used much later by Defoe in *Moll Flanders.*

Greene's success with his efforts to attract readers was partially the result of his use of language that appealed to men and women who were unaware of the fashions of the court and partially the result of the content of the productions themselves. In this genre, Greene is a good representative of the second face of Renaissance style, even if we may doubt the sincerity of his manner of composition. The disappointing element in his achievement is that he stopped writing just as he approached a simple but strong prose for narrative and exposition.

Greene's followers presented similar works to the public well into the seventeenth century and finally became associated with the early character writers. But Thomas Nashe, a university wit who found enjoyment in the arrangement of words, yielded eventually, in *The Unfortunate Traueller. Or, The Life of Jacke Wilton,* of 1593, to the demand for entertainment for the unsophisticated populace. In this instance Nashe tried to demonstrate that real life, as it was seen or read about in current narratives of travelers and historians, was rich and exciting. His story is told by an incorrigible page and linked to events that can be given a date: he proceeded from the beginning, at the siege of Tournay, to the end on the Field of the Cloth of Gold, in the reign of Henry VIII. He seemingly consulted authentic sources so he could relate the fictitious feats of his hero to the real occurrences of that historical period. In this, his only attempt to create what would much later be considered a novel, Nashe developed a way of writing that was entirely his own; and in *Strange News* he defended himself against possible charges of influence from Lyly and Greene: "Did I talk of counterfeit birds, or herbs or stones? This I will proudly boast . . . that the vaine which I have is of my own begetting and calls no man father in England but myself."[18] He had, in fact, turned to the picaresque story, in which the knightly heroes of earlier ages were supplanted by rogues. But Jacke Wilton is not actually a rogue; he lives less by his wits than for the enjoyment of life, and Nashe's narrative is not a fully developed example of the picaresque tale. Its importance lies in the valid use of commonplace life for a rousing story intermingling comic elements with the fearful and the terrifying in a new manner. When Jacke is sold, then, to a physician for anatomical purposes, he describes his sensations in vigorous prose in which the sardonic levity is typical of his best efforts:

> O, the colde sweating cares which I conceived after I
> knewe I should be cut like a French summer dublet. Me

thought already the blood began to gush out at my nose: if a flea on the arme had but bit me, I deemed the instrument had prickt me. Wel, well, I may scoffe at a shrowd turne, but theres no no such readie way to make a man a true Christian, as to perswade himselfe he is taken up for an anatomie. Ile depose I praid then more than I did in seven yeare before. . . . In the night I dreamd of nothing but phlebotomie, bloudie fluxes, incarnatives, running ulcers. I durst not let out a wheale for feare through it I should bleede to death.[19]

Both Thomas Deloney and Thomas Dekker continued to display an interest in the rich vein of depicting life as they saw it, without idealization. The latter, who lived until 1641, completed a few pieces of real artistic merit. But Deloney became known best because of his concern with tradesmen. Although his most memorable successes are to be found only in patches and his highly bred ladies still speak with traces of euphuism, he made the first genuine attempt to portray in fiction the human affairs of people about him. Unlike Greene and Nashe, he was not a university wit; for the greater part of his life he was a silk-weaver at Norwich and a composer of ballads which expressed grievances of the working classes.

Deloney's first attempt, *The Pleasant Historie of John Winchcomb, in his yonguer yeares called Jack of Newbery* (1597), is set in the same period that Nashe chose for *The Unfortunate Traueler*; but whereas Nashe began with Henry VIII's camp during the French expedition of 1513, Deloney chose life among the clothworkers of Newbury, in Yorkshire, in the same era. The result is like a popular biography, describing the gradually increasing success of a tradesman. The eleven chapters are held together by the figure of the shrewd and prosperous weaver, John Winchcomb. He marries the widow of his rich employer and becomes the director of a thriving business. He then equips a company of 250 artisans for war against the Scots in the campaign of Flodden, and performs several acts which add to the glory of the clothworkers, to whom the book is dedicated. Along with some old material, Deloney describes in an original manner a kind of life that Lyly and Sidney had completely avoided.

When some of the wild youths of Newbury scoff at Jack because he refuses to be drawn away from his duties, he has an appropriate answer ready. The dialogue here is typical of Deloney's best writing, even if traces of artificiality remain:

Doubtlesse (quoth one) I thinke some female spirit hath inchaunted *Jacke* to his treadles, and conjured him within the compasse of his Loome, that he can stirre no further.

You say true (quoth *Jacke*) and if you have the leasure to stay till the Charme be done, the space of sixe dayes and five nights, you shall finde me ready to put on my holy-day-apparell, and on Sunday morning for your paines I will give you a pot of Ale over against the Maypole.

Nay (quoth another) Ile lay my life, that as the Salamander cannot live without the fire, so *Jack* cannot live without the smel of his Dames smock.

And I marvell (quoth *Jacke*) that you being of the nature of a Herring (which so soon as he is taken out of the Sea, presently dyes) can live so long with your nose out of the pot.

Nay *Jacke*, leave thy jesting (quoth another) and goe along with us, thou shalt not stay a jot.

And because I will not stay; nor make you a lyer (quoth *Jacke*) Ile keep me here still: and so farewell.[20]

Deloney knew thoroughly the people of whom and for whom he wrote, the inhabitants of the country and the towns of England about the end of the sixteenth century. Although *Jack of Newbery* is one of his best known stories, *Thomas of Reading* is better in construction and equally effective in its method of expression. Written chiefly in a plain, unaffected manner, his books are filled with the natural atmosphere of their settings. Deloney was good, if somewhat superficial, in describing characters, especially in comparison with Lyly, Sidney, and Nashe. Widely read before his death in 1600, his productions attracted large numbers of readers throughout the seventeenth century.

Since the Elizabethans lived in a time of trial and error in the composition of prose, only a few of them, men like Hooker, More, Ralegh, Andrewes, and Donne, along with Tyndale in his translation of the New Testament, were able to combine content and form effectively. Notably absent from this select group are the authors of prose fiction, whose works can scarcely be recognized as masterpieces of English literature. Their value lies in their efforts to develop a satisfactory form of style and expression, although several of their achievements are still enjoyable.[21]

Notes

[1]Esther Cloudman Dunn, *The Literature of Shakespeare's England* (New York, 1936), pp. 164-75.

[2](New York, 1899), p. 4; (London, 1924-39), II, reprinted 1960 (New York, Barnes & Noble, pp. 56, 65-66; *The Growth of the English Novel* (London, 1951), p. 8; *Cavalcade of the English Novel* (New York, 1954 Edition), p. 7; *English Literature in the Sixteenth Century* (Oxford, 1954), p. 351. (*Oxford History of English Literature.*); *The English Novel: A Panorama* (Boston, 1960), p. 25.

[3]*The Complete Works of John Lyly*, ed. R. Warwick Bond (Oxford, 1902), I, 179-80.

[4]Gabriel Harvey is thought to have used the term first, in his *Aduertisement for Papp-hatchett*, where he applied it to Lyly's liking of comparisons taken from an exaggerated natural history. V. Baker, II, 61, n.

[5]For this analysis of the euphuistic style I have relied partially upon Baker, II, 63-64, although other analyses are similar.

[6]*The Complete Works of John Lyly*, I, 251-52.

[7]Baker, II, 66.

[8]Lewis, pp. 312, 314.

[9]*The Prose Works of Sir Philip Sidney*, ed. Albert Feuillerat (Cambridge, Reprinted 1962), I, 3.

[10]Lewis, p. 339.

[11]Lewis, pp. 340-41 elaborates upon this idea.

[12]*The Prose Works of Sir Philip Sidney*, I, 13.

[13]*The Prose Works of Sir Philip Sidney*, III, 10.

[14]George Williamson, *The Senecan Amble* (London, 1951), p. 26, describes this kind of prose.

[15]Sister Miriam Joseph. C.S.C., *Rhetoric in Shakespeare's Time* (New York and Burlingame, 1962), p. 8. (A Harbinger Book.)

[16]Dunn, p. 189.

[17]A. V. Judges, *The Elizabethan Underworld* (London, 1930), pp. 130-31.

[18]Quoted in *Shorter Novels: Elizabethan* (London and New York, 1929), pp. xiv-xv. (Everyman's Library.)

[19]*Shorter Novels: Elizabethan*, p. 339.

[20]*Shorter Novels: Elizabethan*, p. 6.

[21]After this article was completed, a recent book on a related subject came to the writer's attention too late for him to incorporate it into his discussion of style: Wesley Trimpi, *Ben Jonson's Poems: A Study of the Plain Style* (Stanford, Calif., 1962). Mr. Trimpi finds that Elizabethan writers, especially of prose, were subjected by rhetoricians to many pressures about different kinds of style; and furthermore, he supports the conception of the importance of a style of which the glory is to appear as though it were no style, the one here characterized as shapeless, however far the writers of prose fiction may have been from its perfection.

Part V

VARIATIONS ON A THEME IN THE WESTERN TRADITION

It was customary in the early days of my schooling to divide the history of the West into rather sharply defined periods. These sharp divisions had the unquestioned merit of simplifying both the learning and the teaching processes with reference to political and literary history. Precisely how much contact with reality these divisions engendered is quite another matter. My contemporaries may well smile with me at some of the naive assumptions implicit in these old divisions.

In those days of neatly packaged concepts we spoke first of the Ancient World (its history, philosophy, art, and most especially its literature); this period comprised a set of volumes and a set of courses whose termini occurred pedagogically sometime during the first week of June and historically with an event we called "the Fall of Rome." This latter event was associated with Theodoric and his Ostrogoths and, for the convenience of a round number, roughly ascribed to the year A.D. 500. Except for the persecution of the Christians, whose martyrdom and subsequent calendarization somewhat ameliorated the disaster, there was little ill to be said about this period. And, in a literary sense, that judgment was and is quite accurate, no doubt.

Our next sharply defined period, act two in the drama of the West,

83

was an interlude of misery, degradation and ignorance that we called—quite interchangeably and indiscriminately—the Dark Ages or the Middle Ages. And if the curtain fell on act one in the year 500, it rose for act two with admirable exactitude shortly thereafter. On the whole, this was not a pleasant period to study; but, as a welcome recompense to the school boy, not a very difficult one either. There were a few embalmed figures to be identified, an occasional isolated event to attract our attention, and the languid, lazy movement of a few wavy lines across the map of Europe. Its literature, with a few exceptions, was in the cocoon or foetal stage; even the few exceptions were little more than pregnant stirrings of the foetus. This was the period of the long sleep; to borrow a description that may indeed come from the period itself, the fire slept in the hearth; the birds slept in the trees; the flies slept on the wall. Everything, like Sleeping Beauty, awaited the kiss of Prince Charming. Everything awaited the Rebirth, the Renaissance.

With the advent of the Renaissance we and history got busy again. Important things were happening; the long-broken wires were spliced; the circuit had been re-established; the lights were on again. The long wail of the miserere was over; history had made recontact with itself, and the march of enlightenment had resumed its inevitable progress. Thus was the dramatic third act about to begin, an uninterrupted paean of joy.

Viewed dramatically, these periods constituted a most satisfactory achievement in creative activity. We left the theatre that final June with a sense of well-being and satisfaction. For the most part we had seen a well-made play.

A few mechanical difficulties were obvious even then, however. For instance, the curtain had difficulty rising all in one piece on that ecstatic third act. There was no convenient date for the beginning of that third act. That should have provided, even then, a clue to one of our misconceptions: we were trying to establish the Renaissance as a lateral or horizontal event for Western Civilization instead of viewing it as a series of related perpendicular developments in a series of related cultures.

As a practicing teacher I should not wish to do away with our predilection for dividing great masses of historical data into periods; I ask merely that we remain concious that these periods are almost entirely subjective, that they exist not in reality but in our own sense of order and arrangement. Unless we control this order for ourselves, we are likely ourselves to be controlled by someone else's order. As the historian Trevelyan pointed out, "Periods are not facts. They are retrospective conceptions . . . useful to focus attention."[1] Welcoming any increased flexibility in our conception of history, the present Cambridge Professor of

Medieval and Renaissance Literature, C. S. Lewis, comments further, "All lines of demarcation between what we call 'periods' should be subject to constant revision."[2]

One sterotype of my own early days has already been exploded, in the Latin sense of the word. We no longer speak interchangeably of the Dark Ages and the Middle Ages. On this point I should ill use time in applying the whip-lash to a dead horse. For it is now customary to divide into two periods the long years between the fall of Rome and the flowering of the Renaissance. The fashionable division now coincides with the millenium. Thus we have come, somewhat belatedly, to admit into our new concept of the Middle Ages, from about A.D. 1000 on, an enlightenment, a degree of literary excellence, and a general level of civilization in the West for several hundred years preceding the Renaissance. But we would still be doing ourselves an injustice, I believe, to regard the dates 500 to 1000 as indicating limits of a general blanket of darkness covering Western Civilization as a whole.

I think that as we begin to penetrate this predicated area of general darkness we may find: (1) that it did not in fact begin in A.D. 500; (2) that it was neither lateral nor universal in the West; and (3) that it was at most periodic in the individual sub-cultures, interrupted by brilliant flashes. The appellation "Dark Ages" is not precisely applicable to the British Isles during the latter sixth and throughout the entire seventh and eighth centuries. In addition to the work of the Irish, the Welsh, and the Scotch (sacred and profane, in both the Celtic and the Latin tongues), the great monastery universities (and those who are familiar with the many-faceted aspects of the medieval monastery will understand my functional use of the broader term) of England provided other parts of Europe with trained scholars. We would have to admit under the term "Dark Ages" the writings of Boethius in Italy and those of Isidore in Spain. We must, to revert to England, include Caedmon, Bede, and Alcuin. And, before the millenium had been reached, the whole body of Anglo-Saxon literature had been produced, including, the *Beowulf*; and the scholarly work of Alfred and his associates had already been completed. In France we must include Gregory of Tours.

Is it not a curious anomaly that we distinguish the Dark Ages from those we call enlightened by ascribing to the latter a return to classical ways and learning and ascribing to the other the almost complete loss of that learning, when we are faced with the inescapable fact that almost everything that was written on the continent during the Dark Ages was written in the classical tongue, whilst the usual linguistic vehicle for the products of the Renaissance was the individual vernacular?

And lastly there was, during this period of the Dark Ages as we now see them, a great sheet-lightning—the only one in fact that did cover the West laterally; only the profound bias of a modern indifference can fail to understand either its significance or its enlightenment. This was the period of the Christening of Europe. We reach a time in the history of any civilization when first things come first. Such literature as we have from what we call the Dark Ages is of sterling value. If it is not so great in bulk as we might like it to be, that may well be because the best men of the age were busy building the foundations of the house in which literature was to live. Nor was this Dark Age without its technical contributions. Professor Lewis points out that the Dark Ages "saw the triumph of the *codex* or hinged book over the roll or *volumen*—a technical improvement almost as important for the history of learning as the invention of printing. All exact scholarship depends upon it."[3]

From a purely literary viewpoint, the continuity of tradition between what we now call the Dark Ages and the Middle Ages is so marked that it would be impossible to make a meaningful division between these periods at the year 1000 or elsewhere on literary evidence alone. We are forced to make such a division, if at all, in terms of more general considerations. The interested student, who will want to examine the evidence for himself, but who may have difficulties with both the medieval Latin and the vernaculars, should consult that excellent anthology, *Medieval Literature in Translation*, edited by Professor C. W. Jones of California.[4] The very mechanics of his arrangement make this continuity evident and emphasize the national (or ethnic) pecularities as well as the international characteristics of medieval literature.

If the latter portion of the Dark Ages is not easy to delimit, neither is its beginning. The traditional date of A.D. 500 has only one merit: it is a convenient date with which to end a political history of the Western Roman Empire. The classical literature of Rome had long ceased to be produced. Moreover, this date tells us nothing about the general culture of the various peoples of the West at that time.

If we focus our attention on the events immediately following the late fifth century invasion of Italy by Theodoric and his Ostrogoths as the start of the Dark Ages, we are likely to bring to this scene, dramatic as it in fact was, some additional and rather unwarranted dramatic trappings. We are likely to picture the classic lands in terms of Poe's magnificent aphorism, "the glory that was Greece/And the grandeur that was Rome." We are likely to forget that in the late fifth century these attributions no longer held for either with any high degree of accuracy. And we are likely to picture the invaders with all the cruelty and ruthlessness that the term "barbarian" connotes. The trap is an easy one to fall into: what we are likely to come up with is a theatrical representation of virtue most cruelly and violently attacked by vice. I suggest that the fallacy now becomes rather apparent. For it must be obvious, on the most cursory examination of the evidence, that in the fifth century (or considerably earlier, for that matter) neither the Eastern nor the Western Roman Empire was qualified to play the role of sweet, unsullied Little Nell. I know it is no longer fashionable to read the patristic writings, but I recommend a reperusal of St. Augustine's *City of God* as a reasonable contrast to the city of Rome in that century.[5]

The theatrical scene we so often envision has other fallacies as well, if we are to evaluate with any degree of impartiality the respective claims of the Romans and the Germanic invaders to establish and maintain order in Europe. For this was the basic problem, which both failed to meet and solve in terms of their native traditions.

I should state parenthetically that perhaps the least valid of our objections to the stereotyped scene is to recall that these barbarian villains who raped our Little Nell were, if not our direct ancestors, at least closely related to them. It may be the privilege of advanced sophistication to condemn Grandfather for the very heritage we enjoy; but we might first examine the evidence impartially before raising the eye-brow at our own antecedents.

And if we are to be reasonably impartial before rival claims, we cannot honestly begin by accepting the conclusions of one of the litigants. The very term "barbarian" falls into that catagory; as used by the Graeco-Roman world of the fifth century, it is at once a judgment and an epithet used by one people at war with another. Within the reasonable limits of any modern concept of "civilized man," the invading Germans may certainly have failed to qualify; but I suggest that so did the defending Romans, against whom must be imputed the additional charge of cultural degeneration. For this fall from grace—the real fall of the Roman Empire —had been going on for some centuries in both the Eastern and Western portions of that Empire.

Viewed this way, what we call the Dark Ages becomes coincidentally a state of culture, a state of mind, a state of spiritual values, and, if you will, a veritable (low) state of grace, one that began and acquired almost irresistible momentum long before the Visigoths, the Vandals, the Huns or the Ostrogoths funneled through. This internal enveloping darkness had, in fact, created the very low-pressure area that dictated the subsequent path of the invading hurricanes.

Continuing this manner of viewing our tradition, what we call the Middle Ages becomes also a state of culture, a state of mind, a state of spiritual values, and a state of grace; and it expresses itself in the broadest sense as a re-establishment of order: not necessarily the "order" that was Rome's, but a unifying factor that provides a framework within which the sub-cultures can develop individually and collectively, be they Latin, Hellenic, Celtic, Germanic, or Slavic.

If, therefore, we view the Middle Ages as a direction of being, there arises a very reasonable case for beginning them with St. Paul, and thus for their coexisting with, and struggling against, the Dark Ages from the very beginning.

There remains to discuss the fluidity between what we recognize as the latter Middle Ages and the Renaissance proper. If we accept the concept that Western Civilization has never been a single and indivisible unit, but at best a totality of interrelated subcultures permeated and unified by the dogma of the Incarnation, then each subdivision can be conceived of as having had its own Renaissance in relation to and yet independent of each of the others.

At this point it is well to remember that the term "Renaissance" covers a vast range of notions: artistic, intellectual, literary, political, social, and spiritual. This list of elements is not exhaustive, nor are the items mutually exclusive. If considered only from its results, we might profitably follow the example of those German scholars who use the hyphenated term, Renaissance-Reformation. Thus what we call the Renaissance becomes not a single star in the Heavens, but (even to the naked eye) a Doppelstern. With the aid of even the weakest glasses, this in turn becomes (if you will pardon a by-reference to Ronsard and his associates) the Pléiades; stronger glasses will reveal an even greater constellation.

The various directions of expression that the complicated activities of the Renaissance assumed were not the same, perhaps even in mixture of ingredients, and certainly not in emphasis, in the various subcultures of the West. The Doppelstern concept of Renaissance-Reformation is used not to describe a reality, but to emphasize the two dominant ingrediential mixtures, permitting any number of variations between possible extremes. Thus, within limits, it is possible to say that what we commonly regard as the Renaissance focus (as distinguished, however artificially, from the Reformation focus) was the primary manifestation in the southern areas, and that the northern areas were preoccupied primarily with the Reformation focus.

The countries of the happier middle area, primarily France, England,[6] and the German Rheinland, though the degree and direction were different among them, showed a remarkably well-balanced mixture of both.

Yet these two foci had much in common, and what they had in common is what we generally mean by the Renaissance—and the Reformation.

Happily, it is no longer necessary to explain the Renaissance merely as "the rebirth of learning." In the first place, ancient learning had never completely died in the West; and the rediscovery of Catullus hardly explains the feverish activity that was coincident with it. We are on both orthodox and safe ground, I believe, to see the Renaissance-Reformation as (1) the widespread expression of individualism (which is not the same as rejection of established authority, though it often took that form) and (2) the widespread use of a means of contact or communication. The second, of course, was supplied by the printing-press; the former, though less tangible, is no less real. Whence came both? Certainly not from a re-discovery of ancient learning. The ancients of the West had no printing-press, had not in fact even the hinged book. It was not the rediscovery of ancient learning that created the Renaissance (this would be putting the cart before the horse); but, rather, the characteristic attitudes of the men of the Renaissance that demanded an everincreasing search for kindred attitudes expressed in ancient learning.

Whence then came the Renaissance? Unless the men who produced the Renaissance were a momentarily large number of biological mutants or visitors from Mars, we must accept the Renaissance as a very direct and logical outgrowth of the Middle Ages itself. The fact that many producers of the Renaissance, in the exercise of their individualism, broke away, partially or radically, from many established concepts of the Middle Ages merely confirms it. I suggest that you don't "break away" from something unless you are first a part of it; and there will, moreover, be a strong carry-over.

Several dry haystacks may catch fire from one that has ignited first, but each individual fire is based on the composition of its own haystack. In this way each cultural and/or ethnical area of the West had its own Renaissance-Reformation, growing out of and showing the characteristics of its own Middle Ages. Those who produced the Renaissance and whose works are its expression were themselves essentially men and women of the late Middle Ages. Characteristically, they (in common with their predecessors of several hundred years) had two sets of roots: the deep tap roots, reaching into their own historic past and people; and the lateral roots, more or less extensive in each individual case, encompassing some or a great deal of the international or common medieval culture.

Finally, let me comment that much of the dichotomy that we see, or pretend to see, between the Renaissance productions of a given country and its medieval productions may be merely a projection of ourselves and our own way of thinking into the understandably more attractive Renaissance period of that nation. We feel, and commendably, I think, that we are both the heirs and the children of the Renaissance, forgetting that there have been intervening events that may make this no longer a completely tenable belief. It is, then, most natural that we should read into the works of that great period our own sense of values. Let me illustrate this by reference to the works of certainly the greatest figure in the English dramatic Renaissance.

Not too long ago Professor J. E. Uhler of Louisiana discussed Shakespeare's *Julius Caesar* as a morality of "Respublica."[7] To do this he must reject the weight of nineteenth and twentieth century critical interpretation, a complex of interpretations that, for the most part, projects with well-meaning intentions our own political aspirations and philosophy into an Elizabethan play. Professor Uhler sees the play as a tragedy of disrupted order in a state about to enter chaos.

I shall not take up your time with a resumé of the varied critical interpretations of *Hamlet* that have been offered in the past century and a half. They are well represented, except for the more recent ones, in the Furness *Variourm*.[8] Some see Hamlet as a victim of seventeenth century melancholia; others explain him in terms of varying degrees of madness; to still others he is a victim of hyper-sophisticated indecision. The play itself has been treated as an example of the Senecan revenge motif, and there has been considerable discussion as to whether within the meaning of Greek drama the play is a "tragedy" at all. Finally, Hamlet himself has been subjected to Freudian psychoanalysis.

If we think of Shakespeare as a product of the late Middle Ages, then it is possible to examine certain characteristics and beliefs common to many at that time and expect to find expression of them in Shakespeare's own times. This is another way of saying that had Chaucer been able to see *Hamlet* he would more likely have understood what Shakespeare was about than we—or Hazlitt.

What are some of those beliefs, some of which may and some of which may not find acceptance in modern opinion? A few that seem applicable to the play under consideration are: (1) man has an immortal soul that has an independent existence after bodily death; (2) the very real possibility of either Divine or Satanic intervention in human affairs (and this, incidentally, presumes belief in an interested and personal God and also in an interested and personal devil); (3) such intervention may take the form of ghostly apparitions; (4) order, ceremony, and decorum, important as they were in the life of the individual, were even more important in the life of the state; that is, rulers existed for the primary purpose of maintaining order and justice; (5) murder was a deadly and mortal sin, and of all murders regicide was the most heinous; (6) noblesse oblige, especially that people charged by birth or delegation with the protection of the state were no longer free to live their own lives for themselvs; but were directly responsible to God for the discharge of their duties, though' this entail every possible personal sacrifice. We could go on, but these are enough. Any reading of medieval literature will indicate that these were part of the common mores of the West; the fact that some of them were "more honoured in the breach than in the observance" is not especially relevant to the regard in which they were held.

These are all essentially medieval beliefs. In Shakespeare we have a man who presumably holds these beliefs writing for an audience that presumably shares them. Few in number as they are, they are sufficient to explain every major motivation and action of the play. For it begins with a ghostly apparition that informs the hero that he is in very fact the king of Denmark and that the ostensible king is both a usurper and a regicide. As a reasonable and cautious man, fully aware of the wiles of the Devil, Hamlet's real problem is to determine the source of the apparition, and concomitantly to verify the facts of the revelation. If he acts on a Satanic trick he stands to lose his own soul and to do the state an irreparable wrong. If, on the other hand, this apparition is of Divine source, his obligation, at whatever cost to himself, is clear. He must re-establish rightful and legitimate order, so that the consequent death of Claudius is an execution, neither personal murder nor an act of revenge.

With commendable caution he sets out to test the facts, and he does so with both the patience and the trials of Job. In the process he suffers loss of friends, family (including his betrothed), and finally his own life. But he has successfully discharged his responsibilities. Within the medieval framework of order and decorum, he has been eminently correct—if not always eminently efficient.

Is this a tragedy? I am not certain that such a question may not imply a quibbling with words. If the man who wrote this play was a man of the late Middle Ages, he was not concerned primarily with Hellenic concepts of tragedy; his sense of values would be rooted elsewhere. He was, instead and more likely, a late medieval Christian, thinking and writing as one.

If I am correct in assuming that the essential element of a Greek tragedy concerns a representative man, generally of exaggerated stature, rebelling against the moral order only to be destroyed by it, then *Hamlet* is not by that standard a "tragedy." For Hamlet is neither a man of exaggerated stature, nor is he rebelling against the moral order. He has fulfilled his mission; in death he is very properly escorted by "flights of angels." In the Greek sense there can be no tragedy for a Christian hero. Rather does the play reveal its author as a legitimist, whose hero achieves by every possible sacrifice the restitution of order, decorum and peace. These were the basic ideals of the Middle Ages, and they are properly expressed in the greatest play of the English Renaissance.

Notes

[1]C. M. Trevelyn, *English Social History*, London, 1944, p. 92.

[2]C. S. Lewis, *De Descriptione Temporum*, Cambridge University Press, 1955, p. 3.

[3]*Ibid.*, p. 8.

[4]Charles W. Jones, *Mediaeval Literature in Translation*, New York, Longmans, Green and Co., 1950.

[5]Written, by the way, as the result of an earlier Germanic invasion, that of A.D. 410.

[6]Scotland must be included with the northern areas.

[7]John Earle Uhler, "Julius Caesar — a Morality of Respublica," *Studies in Shakespeare*, University of Miami Press, 1953; pp. 96-106.

[8]More recent coverage is discussed by R. M. Smith, "Current Fashions in Hamlet Criticism," *Shakespeare Association Bulletin*, vol. 29 (Jan. 1949), pp. 11-22; Earnest Brenecke, "All Kinds of Shakespeare," *Shakespeare Quarterly*, vol. 1, pp. 272-80; H. D. Grey, "Some Methods of Approach to the Study of Hamlet," *Studies in Philology*, vol. 45 (1948), pp. 203-15; and in Hardin Craig's two longer studies, *An Interpretation of Shakespeare* and *The Enchanted Glass*.

Part VI

A STUDY OF TAFFETA PHRASES . . . AND HONEST KERSHEY NOES[1]

When the Cambridge editors began their introduction to Love's Labour's Lost[2] with the observation that critics had dealt harshly with this play and commentators neglectingly, their statement was probably truer then than today. Yet there perisists in criticism somewhat of indifference to the play's formal rhetorical devices. With but few exceptions[3] this disregard continues in spite of the fact that it has long been a commonplace to state as indeed does the title page of the 1598 Quarto itself that this is 'A pleasant Conceited Comedie'.[4]

This study will attempt to show by examination of Berowne's allegory[5] and Rosaline's quips preceding and following it (V, ii, 395-416) a relationship between the textile terms and the sixteenth century English trade with Muscovy, linking this passage to the masque of the Muscovites earlier in the scene. Meanings of the terms, now grown dim, as well as Rosaline's rebuke suggest that Berowne's forswearing of rhetorical ornament is rather assumed[6] than actual and that he is consciously ordering his seige of Rosaline upon the Quintilian[7] (and Ciceronian) principle of oratorical propriety. For Quintilian says (XI, i, 2): ". . . since the ornaments of style are varied and manifold and suited to different purposes, they will, unless adapted to the matter and the persons concerned, not merely fail to give our style distinction, but will even destroy its effect and produce a result quite the reverse of that which our matter would produce." Berowne appears to be adapting to the matter—his predicament and his love—and to the person: Rosaline,

> A whitely wanton with a velvet brow,
> With two pitch balls stuck in her face for eyes.
>
> (III, i, 195-196)

The King, Berowne, and the two other young lords attending upon Navarre have returned to pay a ceremonious call upon the Princess and her young ladies whom these same courtiers have but lately visited as 'a mess of Russians' or as Rosaline put it "Disguised like Muscovites, in shapeless gear." The truth is beginning to be borne in upon the young lords that all has been discovered. The King fears they will be mocked downright. Dumaine would confess and turn all into a jest, but Rosaline's quip pins at least one of these soldiers of Saint Cupid to his predicament:

> Help, hold his brows, he'll swoon . . . Why look you so pale?
> Sea-sick, I think, coming from Muscovy.
>
> (V, ii, 393-394)

There was much to make Shakespeare aware of Muscovy in the late eighties and nineties. The publication of the only known Quarto in 1598 combined with Meres' mention in *Palladis Tamia* in the same year gives an end date within the nineties decade in the puzzling question of the dating of the play. Even though a wide diversity of opinion concerning the date of composition has existed[8] and still exists, ranging from 1588 to 1596/7, James G. McManaway suggests that "it appears wiser as yet to retain the more conservative date of 1594/5."[9] Since this study is not primarily concerned with an exact dating—however desirable that might be—the loose diversity of the decade from 1588 to 1598 will suffice; 1589 saw the publication of the shorter version of Hakluyt's great work and 1598 began the publication of the three volume edition of *The Principal Voyages, Traffiques & Discoveries of the English Nation* (1598-1600).[10]

It is no new thing to refer the reader to Hakluyt as a source for Shakespeare; in fact, Frederick C. Sorenson[11] cites *The Principal Navigations* (1589) as a possible source for the descriptions of Russia and Russian costumes in the Masque of the Muscovites. But it is not the descriptions of Russian costumes, or even of Russia itself, that are most pertinent in Hakluyt to a study of Berowne's textile allegory: rather the full accounts and letters concerning the lively merchants trade between England and Russia. Now that trade was in many commodities, and important among them were kersies and russets from England and silk from Persia brought overland into Russia and thence at last by ship to London or other English port.[12] Even without Hakluyt this trade could have been no great secret. Something more than a quarter of a century ago, E. K. Chambers observed that the Muscovite Masque reflects an English interest in Russian affairs.[13] Later Sarah M. Nutt writing of the monopoly held by the Muscovy Company in trade via the Arctic and the White Sea states that "Shakespeare no doubt reflects this English interest in Russia in *Love's Labour's Lost* (Act 5, scene 2)."[14] Robert Ralston Cawley in *The Voyagers and Elizabethan Drama* points out that Lee, Hart, and the earlier Ritson have sought to draw a Russian political or masque parallel to Shakespeare's Muscovites.[15] But so far as I have been able to determine no one has noted a relationship between the hazardous trade with Musco and the textile terms of Berowne's allegory.

The Muscovy Company had first received their charter in 1555— that is, 1 and 2 Philip and Mary. That same year Richard Chancellor had laid the foundation of the commerce which became of such importance to both England and Russia. For this trade, craftsmen of the English cloth guilds had been industriously preparing russets, kersies, and other textiles.[16]

That the trek both by sea and over land was dangerous, the 1589 Hakluyt made Englishmen aware through the thrilling accounts of the *Edward Bonaventure* in which Chancellor discovered the White Sea, then called the Bay of St. Nicholas, while hoping to find a Northeast route by which men might pass from Russia to Cathaia. Those who stayed home must have pondered upon the mutability of man's existence when they learned of the perishing of Sir Hugh Willoughby in the frozen North even while Chancellor pushed through to Moscow, only to be himself drowned on the return voyage in a second expedition when his vessel was wrecked off Scotland. The Russian ambassador Osep Napea was on that voyage but escaped death, finally arriving in London to be most courteously received.[17] The reader wonders if the young lords of *Love's Labour's Lost* may not have chosen to entertain their ladies with a masque of Muscovites, in part at least, because the lords were themselves aware that their perjured vows had thrust them into a perilous expedition of love. At any rate Rosaline, by her quip, must sometime have heard of rough weather encountered coming from Muscovy.[18]

That Shakespeare and Berowne derive considerable from Quintilian, T. W. Baldwin has made clear. His study is wide enough in scope to include discussion of several passages of *Love's Labour's Lost*. Relative to this present study is his exposition of Berowne's use of hyperbole in the taffeta phrases passage which evidences that Shakespeare knew Quintilian's definition of hyperbole, including the dangerous relation it bore to *affectatio,* a vice of language. Baldwin asserts that so far as he has been able to find only in Quintilian does this full pattern occur. Shakespeare not only has demonstrated his knowledge of the Quintilian categories of rhetoric but has caught their significance as well.[19]

Now Berowne was left some pages back in this study staggering up from Rosaline's quip about coming sea-sick from Muscovy. It is of consequence to the tone of the whole passage that he answers her in the first six lines in terms of warfare. The stars pour down plagues for perjury as if from a battlement. He asks if any face of brass could hold longer out as though his arsenal of wit were quite gone. Ammunition exhausted, or so he seems to say, he stands before her stubbornly to endure her bruising scorn, her flouting wit which darts and cuts to pieces with a keen conceit. It is interesting to observe that just as Berowne is getting his second wind that it is to rhetorical terms that he resorts in analyzing just what has happened to him: first, the flout, what Puttenham calls the broad flout—that is, *antiphrasis.* Here Berowne is apparently referring to the colloquy just past in which Rosaline has said the opposite of what she has implied (V, ii, 371-372) and, when reproved by Berowne, has cleverly started an *antiphrasis* which he is forced to cap, thus convicting himself of being a fool. The *conceit* which he next mentions refers directly to the "Sea-sick, I think, coming from Muscovy."

Berowne has suited the style to the matter and apparently to the person, for Rosaline is at least listening. The next six lines move into an easier slower rhythm as if the speaker were beginning to breathe more regularly:

> And I will wish thee never more to dance,
> Nor never more in Russian habit wait.
> O, never will I trust to speeches penned,
> Nor to the motion of a schoolboy's tongue,
> Never come in vizard to my friend,
> Nor woo in rhyme, like a blind harper's song.
> (V, ii, 400-405)

While Berowne is meticulously itemizing the things he never more will do, each of them related either to the masque of the Muscovites or to the previous sonnet writing, he is accomplishing at least three ends. He is keeping Rosaline from confounding him with a flout, making confession of wrong-doing—if not implying willingness to do penance, and, last, allowing himself time to gather his rhetorical powers.

Taffeta phrases, silken terms precise,
    Three-piled hyperboles, spruce affections,
Figures pedantical—these summer-flies
    Have blown me full of maggot ostentation.
I do forswear them, and I here protest,
    By this white glove
        (how white the hand, God knows!)
Henceforth my wooing mind shall be expressed
    In russet yeas and honest kersey noes.
And, to begin, wench—so God help me, la!—
    My love to thee is sound, sans crack or flaw.
                 (V, ii, 406-415)

To which Rosaline, who is not for the first time experiencing the sweet smoke of rhetoric, darts her skill with

            Sans 'sans', I pray you.
                      (V, ii, 416)

    Berowne's speech above may not be the proud full sail of his great verse in the salve for perjury argument (IV, iii, 217f) but hardly does Berowne now appear other than a man in control of his rhetoric, if not wholly of his love and his lady. Notwithstanding, the artful Rosaline has parried by accusing him of being guilty of an abuse of language called by Puttenham the *soraismus*, or mingle-mangle.[20] The affected and unnecessary use of French *sans* coupled to the common English *crack* and *flaw* occasions her overt thrust. But in this duel of wits the darkly beautiful Rosaline may also be putting Berowne on guard that she has recognized his feint in employing the word *crack*, for it has not only the meanings of break, rift, fissure but others applicable as well. The OED (sb, 4) tells us that *crack* meant: loud talk, a boast, a brag, an exaggeration or a lie, and that in this sense, in the sixteenth century, there was a tendency to use *crake*. The difference in pronunciation scarcely is great enough to preclude a pun. Now the OED also furnished the information that *crake* in Northern dialectic meant crow or raven and in general verbal use meant to utter a harsh grating cry as that of a crow, as John Florio used it in *Second Fruites* "When the Crow begins to crake, The Fox beguiles him of his cake," a couplet perhaps not unknown to Shakespeare's first audience for this play.[21] It would seem that Berowne has rallied and that he has availed himself of Quintilian's wisdom (IX, i, 20-21) that the skilful orator as the skilful swordsman neither always openly attacks nor is without guile.

    Rosaline could but have been aware of other discrepancies between Berowne's statement and his actual behavior. In spite of his prophecy that he will no more woo in rhyme like the blind harper's song, he continues to speak in alternately rhyming lines until he comes to the last two which are, for good measure, a couplet. A further discrepancy is that the "taffeta phrases" speech is not only an allegory but within that large figure employs epithet, metaphor, hyperbole, and other figures, coming close to *tapinosis*, or the abaser (Puttenham, 259) in "summer flies" and "maggot ostentation." Berowne's forswearing is not wholly convincing. Even he admits that he yet has a trick of the old rage, but in the very act of promising to leave it by degrees he launches into another allegory of love and the plague, again rhyming the lines alternately. The whole is full of those turns of speech so much admired of Quintilian, who called *metaphor* the most beautiful of tropes, which "shines forth with a light all its own." (VIII, vi, 4) Berowne, then, exhibits no real penitence for the continued use of rhetoric; in fact, a careful reading of the rest of the fifth act reveals what Walter Pater long ago intuitively felt that Berowne continues to experiment with language,[22] the master weapon by which his wooing mind would gain ascendancy over his lady.

It is from the first allegory that chiefly has stemmed the conception that Berowne does forswear three-piled hyperboles for plain honest words. And the words on which this point of view really seats itself are russet and kersey. Yet the very first word the reader encounters in this textile allegory is taffeta, from Persian *taftah*, a thin fine silk fabric of even texture made in many colors and changeable.[23] Furthermore the reader here encounters taffeta not for the first time in this scene, for Boyet "wit's pedler" has uttered the word in the second line after the entrance of the masked Muscovites, interrupting the prologue of the young Moth with "Beauties no richer than rich taffeta" (V, ii, 159). Whether the textile allegory in relation of its terms to the Muskovy trade had here begun to form in Shakespeare's mind, or already had formed, is a teasing question incapable of exact proof. But both Folio and Quarto provide us with this juxtaposition of Muskovy and taffeta. Of considerable interest is the fact that the Quarto gives this speech to "Berow"; but since Theobald's assigning it to Boyet, most editors have followed him.[24] Hakluyt furnishes the information that six attempts were made by the Muscovy Company to establish trade with Persia through Russia, extending from 1557 to 1579-81.

Letters from the voyagers to the company indicate the increasing volume and importance of the trade in kersies. From Arthur Edwards on the third voyage to Persia, begun in 1565, there came a letter to the Secretary of the Muscovy Company (Hakluyt, 1589, 376) which notes thirty-two packs of "carseis"[25] as all of that kind of cloth that would be needed. In a letter written April 26, 1566 in Shamakie, Medea, to the right worshipful Sir Thomas Lodge, knight and alderman, Edwards mentions as commodities to be taken out of England: Carseis, tinne, brasil, red cloth, and copper; among commodities to be brought back to England: raw silk, numerous spices, and yew for bow staves.[26] Five hundred pieces of Hampshire kersies were shipped to Russia in 1567 (Hakluyt, 1599, i. 297). On the fourth voyage made by Master Edwards, he is calling for a thousand "karsies," in his letter to the company April 28, 1569.[27] In addition to the trade letters are those of Queen Elizabeth which evince her interest in the voyages to Russia and Persia both for their trade and political importance.[28]

As increasing volume of kersies marked the progress of the Muscovy trade, so contrasting commodities have often been thought to make Berowne's textile allegory. After taffeta phrases are found silken terms precise, such perhaps as satin, sarcenet, three-piled velvet, or even tuft-taffeta,[29] the tufts of which like Berowne's hyperboles were piled high, only to be followed by russet yeas and honest kersey noes. The usual gloss at this point is for *russet:* simple, homespun; and for kersey: plain, homely; or so far as the gloss and notes are concerned, the rest is silence. The OED states that kersey is a kind of coarse, narrow cloth woven from long wool and usually ribbed. Fairholt's Glossary adds that kersey was sometimes of fine fabric, and used for better purposes, and was of Flanders dye and French puce. Linthicum's *Costume* (79) emphasizes the color, describing kersey as a light-weight wool cloth in black, sky, Flanders dye, yellow, sad green, and sheep. Russet, she says, was a dusky reddish brown or ashy-grey and like pure blue symbolized steadfastness. Master Edwards, writing to the Muscovy Company June 16, 1567, from Astracan itemizes an order for the Shaugh of Persia for all sorts and colors of cloths, kersies among them, and London russets "lively to the sight."[30]

Yet by the fifteen-eighties fashions in cloth had begun to change somewhat in London. The new draperies were woven of worsted mixed with flax or silk. As they were softer and of finer texture they began to supplant the old draperies of broadcloth, kersey, penistone, and russet. The fine old kersies began to give place to a narrower, shorter length of cloth, sometimes with a wide selvedge or list.[31]

What is the twentieth century reader to make of such diversity of scope for kersey and russet? Hardly may he rest in peace that they were merely rough homespun grey or brown in color connoting that Berowne would use only plain terms henceforth. For we find that russet and kersey mean color in various degrees, lively to the sight; mean warmth and durability, perhaps, even steadfastness or (as in the later kersies) its reverse. Moreover we have seen them as goods of exchange in trade with

Russia: English weaves, made of English wool by English hands; whereas the silks and velvets are of imported stuff and made by foreign craftsmen, Bergundian, Dutch and French.[32] At least Berowne's textile terms do not necessarily go from fitness for high style to harmony with low style. There is richness of texture in each of the terms, though each differs from each suiting the matter, the person, and the occasion. For Berowne come but late from Muscovy in sorry state is bent on using all the resources of his rhetoric then and throughout to win the whitely wanton who so besets his thoughts. She who knows that a jest's prosperity lies in the ear of him that hears it is not likely to miss or to be wholly unmoved by Berowne's subtleties.

Naturally question arises concerning the effect of Berowne's refusal to forswear rhetoric upon the outcome of the comedy. Is there any relationship between his lack of forswearing and the task which Rosaline near the end of the play imposes upon him? Why did Berowne keep on in his accustomed way, and was Rosaline's apparent objection to his figurative and elaborate language, just that? Her speech as well as his declares, like that of the other lords and ladies, that all have been trained in the courtly tradition of elegant and imaginative language. If Rosaline does object, then she has changed during the course of the play. For in (II, i, 61) when Katherine recalls having met Dumaine at the Duke of Alanson's once and praises him as one whom all that virtue love for virtue loved, Rosaline counters with her own remembrance of Berowne, whom she had met upon that same occasion. Greatly she extols his becoming mirth: his fair tongue is conceit's expositor so that aged ears play truant at his tales and younger hearings are ravished quite.

This conversation has gone on while the Princess and her ladies wait like humble visaged suitors the high will of the King, rumors of whose vow have reached the visitors from France. Evidently the young ladies have been well pleased with Navarre's courtiers at first meeting but now are in the embarrassing situation of finding themselves barred from the little Academe devoted to fasting and study without the comfort of sleep or woman-kind. Of course the guests are courteously lodged, though without gates, and before long each lord has been bewitched to break his oath and to turn sonnet. Fairings are tendered by each vow-breaker and accompanied by the best he has been able to muster up in poetry. The ladies recognizing the perjury and the ineptness of the sonnet writing, set about to mock those considered to have mocked them. Rosaline in particular has it in for Berowne:

> That same Berowne I'll torture before I go
> O, that I knew that he were in by th' week

How I would make him fawn, and beg, and seek,
And wait the season, and observe the times,
And spend his prodigal wits in bootless rhymes
And shape his service wholly at my hests
And make him proud to make me proud, that jests!
So planet—like [Q. 'perttaunt like']
    would I o'er sway his state
That he should be my fool, and I his fate.
                      (V, ii, 60-68)

Perhaps it is right, as the Princess says, that they should mock their lovers so, but in Rosaline surely the lady protests too much. Not only is she not sure that Berowne is in by the week (well caught, say the Cambridge editors), but a certain intensity of zeal to humble him alerts the audience to realize that Rosaline may herself be struggling in Cupid's snares. There seems to be more of anger than jest behind her words, sharpened by Berowne's sonnet which is not wholly in the liver-vein, making flesh a deity.

Hard upon this plot to discomfort the suitors comes Boyet to spread the word of the approach of the maskers. The Princess and her retinue change favors, and themselves masked, entertain the Muscovites, until they are all dry-beaten with pure scoff.

No wonder when later returned with the others, undisguised, Berowne again experiencing an arsenal of wit thinks that the stars pour down plagues for perjury. But Berowne is a highly trained courtier, a conscious and sophisticated rhetorician. He loves this whitely wanton and would get the upper hand of her in this war of words, taming his language to his will and desire. When he lapses in his presumed forswearing abruptly into the ordinary and citizen terms of

    . . . . wench—so God help me, la!
                    (V, ii, 414)

not only does he hope they will ring as rhetorically false upon the ear of his lady as upon his own but also overtly reminds her that she is basically woman, Eve, created to mate no matter how white her courtly hand. Having made his point to one whom he believes as quick in sense as he, he launches into the soraismus. Then tripped up by Rosaline, he sweeps back into the comparative safety of a cool rhetorical plea that the ladies be merciful to those who have caught the plague—and from their eyes. But the ladies do not let their supposed mockers off so easily, fencing them in with "a readie livelinesse of wit, whereby . . . [the lady attending at court] may declare herself far wide of all dullnessse; but with such a kinde of goodnesse that she may bee esteemed no lesse chaste, wise, and courteous than pleasant, feate conceited and sober . . ."[33]

This love-game dialogue is rounded to a finish and upon it comes the show of the Nine Worthies. Over it the crackle of Berowne's wit runs anew like a merciless whip. Scarcely does the humbleness of Costard, realizing that he has "made a little fault in Great" deter Berowne's buoyancy as the satiric commentator on the action. The other lords and the king join in, completely throwing the none too sure Worthies off their speeches, presumably penned by Holofernes, with suggestions by Armado. Not even Alisander's being a marvelous good neighbor, though a little o'er parted daunts the tormentors. When Judas Maccabeus comes on, the Princess herself, though more gently, enters into the fun of routing the ill-rehearsed amateurs. However, it is to be noted that not once does Rosaline open her lips to caustic comment which has previously so readily been provoked from them.

When Hector the quite overcharged armipotent Mars and Pompey, the Huge, have nearly come to blows over Jaquenetta upon whom Nature has already too much intruded, the merriment still goes on among the commentators who are moved only to further quipping by the plight of the poverty-stricken Armado who cannot take off his shirt to fight, as advised, for the simple reason that he goes woolward for penance. Still Rosaline utters no word.

Moth (or perhaps Boyet) cracks the whip of his little wit once more at the expense of Armado. The whirligig of time seems to have stopped in laughter but has not. Harshly arrives the news of the death of the King of France, the Princess' father. Armado breathes free, but the new-sad soul of the Princess prompts her from a heavy heart to bid farewell. Vainly Navarre would prevent it, with Claudius-like comfort that it is more wholesome-profitable to rejoice in new found friends than to wail those lost. Berowne recognizing the clumsiness of the argument states that

> Honest plain words best pierce the ear of grief.
> (V, ii, 414)

but takes off into another flight of rhetoric trying once more speciously to show that what seems like perjury and idle jest, sin brought on by the beauties of the ladies so has purified itself and turned to grace. Again no word is there of true understanding of grief. Magnificently the Princess controls herself, as one less royal than she, might remember her lessons out of the courtesy books. She is gentle, sweet, and witty; no harm has been done; all was merriment and taken so. But Longaville and Dumaine will not leave it at that; their letters and looks have shown much more than jest. For the first time Rosaline speaks, and tersely:

> We did not quote them so.
>
> (V, ii, 783)

She says no more until some thirty lines later she begins to lay upon Berowne the task that he must accomplish to win her. She, and she alone, sends her knight upon a quest; although the Princess' urging of Navarre to spend a year and a day in an hermitage before returning to her is cousin-germane to it.

As has been many times observed, *Love's Labour's Lost* is a complex play. Posed continuously throughout is the question of what is the proper end of study. Although Rosaline had not been present when Berowne opined that study, like heaven's glorious sun will not be deep-searched with saucy looks, yet she has now sent him for a twelve month to an Academe far more severe than that planned by Navarre. One may legitimately ask why the witty, high-spirited Rosaline who was first attracted to her love by the brilliance of his becoming mirth should expose it to so painful a task that, in one of the finest metaphors of the play, he should cry out to her:

> To move wild laughter in the throat of death
> It cannot be, it is impossible.
> Mirth cannot move a soul in extasy.
>
> (V, ii, 851-53)

Frances A. Yates has made clear that love was one of the prime subjects of the Italian Renaissance. Further, she was convinced that Shakespeare knew Bruno's *De gli eroici furori* at least second or third hand and knew at first hand the dialogues of Florio's *Seconde Fruites* which draw from it.[34] Whether Shakespeare was familiar with Bruno's love treatise or not, Sir Thomas Hoby's translation of Castiglione's *The Book of the Courtier* was certainly available. In the Fourth Book, the subject of love comes under discussion. After he has set forth that "Love is nothing else but a certain coveting to enjoy beauty" and that in order to covet we must know, Maister Peter Bembo has the following to add:

> And because in our souls there be three manner waies to know, namely sense, reason, and understanding: of sense ariseth appetite or longing which is common to us with brute beasts; of reason ariseth election or choice, which is proper to man; of understanding, by which man may be partner with the Angels, ariseth will[35]

If Rosaline's mind is moving along lines similar to these during the tormenting of the Nine Worthies, then quite logically she would place the kind of task that she finally does upon Berowne, for he is lacking in the third manner of knowing and his gibing spirit needs to be instructed by grief. He has allowed his reason to lean toward the first way and has perjured his vow, moved by the eyes and person of Rosaline. However, by his wit he has shown the knowledge of letters and language deemed essential for the courtier, thereby giving hope that if that gibing spirit be choked, he may gain the understanding which he now has not.

If Rosaline (and so Shakespeare) knew the theory of *The Courtier* we should find ourselves returning to familiar ground. Earlier in this study we have seen Quintilian citing Cicero's *De Oratore* as authority, and Hoby in his Epistle to Lord Hastings points to the parallels in structure and subject matter between that revered work and Castiglione's *Courtier*. If on the other hand, Shakespeare knew none of the love treatises or the courtesy books, religious instruction being what it was, he could not have escaped Corinthians I, 13:

> Though I speak with the tongues of men and of angels and have not charity, I am become as sounding brass, a tinkling cymbal. . . .
> Charity suffereth long and is kind.

At all odds the dark-eyed Rosaline seemed to have grasped what Castiglione implied (304) that man is caught between the extremes of sense and understanding and that as he leans toward the one or the other he determines what he will become.[36]

The ending of *Love's Labour's Lost* has been a hard one for critics. Berowne himself declares that the play ends not like a comedy; Jack hath not Jill. There have been attempts to explain this ending; doubtless there will be many more, as the shift in mood in the last part of act five calls for analysis of the reason behind this change. The highly rhetorical language of this comedy seems a likely place to find the solution whether one sails the rough seas from Muskovy or sits quietly by the fire with a book while roasted crabs hiss in the bowl. The seasons continue to keep customary pace; Heims follows Ver.

To see Berowne as forswearing taffeta phrases or the precision of silken terms is to miss one of Shakespeare's subtleties. Berowne as courtier must keep the polished rapier of his wit. He knows it and so does Rosaline; but, as she so quickly learns, he must not use it as a loose grace. Rather, even if he be set upon a harsh quest, he must discipline himself to *sprezzatura*, the true grace of the courtier, made up in large part of understanding, other things being equal. Within this skillful and brilliant comedy lies a grasp of *humanitas* as securely as in St. Paul, Cicero, Quintilian, Bruno, or Castiglione,[37] any of whom may have sifted into the making of it.

Notes

[1]This article is an expanded version of the paper read at the Twenty-seventh Annual Meeting of the South Atlantic Modern Language Association at Chattanooga, Tennessee, November 29, 1957.

[2]*The Works of Shakespeare*, ed. by Sir Arthur Quiller-Couch and John Dover Wilson (Cambridge, 1923), vii. Textual reference to *Loves Labour's Lost* is to this edition throughout.

[3]Notable among these is Thomas Whitefield Baldwin, *William Shakespeare's Small Latine and Lesse Greeke*, 2 vols (Urbana, 1944), II, 197-238 and *passim*. But see, also, Weston Babcock, "Fools, Fowls, and Perttaunt-Like in *Love's Labour's Lost*", SQ II (July, 1951); Sister Miriam Joseph, *Shakespeare's Use of the Arts of Language* (New York, 1947); Caroline F. E. Spurgeon, *Shakespeare's Imagery and What it Tells Us* (Cambridge, 1936), throughtout in both these works; W. Schrickx, *Shakespeare's Early Contemporaries*, Antwerpen, 1956, ch. ix.

[4]*Love's Labour's Lost*, 1598, ed. by Sir Walter Greg Shakespeare Quarto Facsimiles, No. 10 (Oxford, 1957).

[5]*The Arte of English Poesie*, ed. by Gladys Doidge Willcock and Alice Walker (Cambridge, 1936), 187. See also John Hoskins, *Dirctions for Speech and Style*, ed. by Hoyt H. Hudson (Princeton, 1935), 9-10. Thomas Cooper, *Eliotes Dictionarie* (1559) gives: "*Allegoria*— a figure called inversion, where it is one in woordes and another in sentence or meaning", as quoted in Joshua McClennen, *On the Meaning and Function of Allegory in the English Renaissance*, Contributions in Modern Philology, Univ. of Mich. Press, No. 6 (April, 1947), 3.

[6]Israel Gollancz, LLL, *The Works of Shakespeare* (London, 1889), II, preface, identifies Shakespeare with Biron alleging that he is 'Shakespeare's own mouthpiece' when forswearing taffeta phrases. Walter Pater, *Appreciations* (London, 1890), 175 says that it is hard not to identify Shakespeare with Biron. For similar assumption see Harley Granville-Barker, *Prefaces to Shakespeare*, 2 vols. (Princeton, 1947), II, 20. Baldwin, II, 231 makes no identification of Shakespeare and Berowne but does agree that "Berowne forswears all the arts of rhetoric and proposes to woo only in 'russet yeas and honest kersey noes' ". David Lloyd Stevenson, *The Love-Game Comedy* (New York, 1946), 191-198 emphasizes 'the perspicacious, plain-speaking Berowne.' E. C. Pettet, *Shakespeare and the Romantic Tradition* (London, 1947), 108 sees Berowne not only as forswearing an artificial type of love-verse but all wooing.

[7]*Institutio Oratoria of Quintilian*, with an English tr. by H. E. Butler, 4 vols. (London, 1921), IV, 155-157 (XI, I, 3-6) in which Quintilian defines propriety and refers it to Cicero, De Oratore, III, x, 37.

[8]LLL, 125. See also Frederick Gard Fleay, *A Chronicle History of the Life and Work of William Shakespeare* (London, 1886), 202.

[9]"Recent Studies in Shakespeare's Chronology, "*Shakespeare Survey*, III Cambridge, 1950), 25. For England's marked political activity in Russia in 1592, see H. B. Charlton, "The Date of *Love's Labour's Lost*, "MLR, XII (July and October, 1918), 257-266 and 317-400. For dating based on topical reference, see Frances A. Yates, *A Study of Love's Labour's Lost* (Cambridge, 1936). Schrickx, *Early Contemporaries*, argues throughout from the Harvey-Nashe controversy for 1592. Alfred Harbage, "*Love's*

Labor's Lost and the Early Shakespeare," PQ, 41 (Jan., 1962), 18-36 denies the Harvey-Nashe quarrel as pertinent and prefers 1588-89 for date on grounds that LLL is a chorister play.

[10]V. De Sola Pinto, The English Renaissance: 1510-1688 (New York, 1918), 201.

[11]"Masque of the Muscovites," MLN, 50 (Dec., 1935), 499-501. Sorenson would include as source Holinshed's account of the Russian Masque performed before Henry VII in which there were blackmoors.

[12]*Early Voyages and Travels to Russia and Persia by Anthony Jenkinson and other Englishmen and some account of the first intercourse of the English with Russia and Central Asia by way of the Caspian Sea*, ed by E. Delmar Morgan and C. H. Coote, Printed for the Hakluyt Society, 2 vols., (London, 1886), I and II, *passim*.

[13]*William Shakespeare: a Study of Facts and Problems*, 2 vols.,(Oxford, 1930) I, 336.

[14]"The Arctic Voyages of William Barents in Probable Relation to Certain of Shakespeare's Plays", SP, XXXIX (April, 1942), 243.

[15](Boston and London, 1938), 263n.

[16]*Early Voyages*, I, iv.

[17]*Early Voyages*, I, ii.

[18]If anything further were needed to make Shakespeare aware of Russia, it could have been furnished by the account by Edward Webbe, a chief master gunner, *Webbe, His Travailes* (1590), reprinted by Edward Arber (London, May 1868). The name of Webbe was not unfamiliar to Shakespeare, for his cousin Robert Webbe lived in Snitterfield . Edgar L. Fripp, *Shakespeare's Haunts Near Stratford* (London, 1929), 19, 95 claims that there was a brother Edward to whom the father Alexander left a legacy of ten pounds; but Chambers (II, xvi) does not include Edward in the lineage of Shakespeare and Arden, setting up Robert only as the son of Margaret Arden and Alexander Webbe. Both Fripp and Chambers (II, 14) recognize John Shakespeare as the overseer of Alexander Webbe's will. There seems, however, to be no evidence to connect the chief master gunner with the Arden-Webbe family.

[19]*Small Latin*, II, 231.

[20]Vere 1. Rubel, *Poetic Diction in the English Renaissance*, MLN Revolving Fund Series XII (London, 1941), 289 and Puttenham, 252-253.

[21]G. B. Harrison, *Shakespeare Under Elizabeth* (New York, 1933) upholds the view that LLL was written to amuse Southampton and his friends. Florio was tutor to Southampton in modern language, especially Italian. See Yates, 3.

[22]*Appreciations*, 172-175.

[23]Marie C. Linthicum, *Costume in the Drama of Shakespeare and his Contemporaries* (Oxford, 1936), 123-124. See also the OED: Taffeta, a name applied to different fabrics at different times. In early times apparently a plain-woven glossy silk (of any color) . . . B2fif, Florid, bombastic, overdressed, dainty, delicate, fastidious . . .

[24]LLL, 172. See also W. W. Greg, *The Editorial Problem in Shakespeare* (Oxford, 1951), 127, for his theory that the Quarto was printed from Shakespeare's foul papers.

[25]*Early Voyages*, I, 382.

[26]*Early Voyages*, II, 392.

[27]*Early Voyages*, II, 407-414.

[28]Such as her correspondence to the Tzar (Charlton, 387-388) and her letter to the Sophie of Persia entrusted to Master Anthony Jenkinson, dated April 26, 1561 from London, *Early Voyages*, I, 112-113.

[29]Linthicum, 66; 124-125 and *Fairholt's Costume in England: A History of Dress to the End of the Eighteenth Century,* ed. by H. A. Dillon (London, 1910), II, 393, 405.

[30]*Early Voyages,* II. 405-406.

[31]Linthicum, 53-60 and 80.

[32]C. L. Barber, *Shakespeare's Festive Comedy,* (Princeton, 1959), 108 does cast somewhat of doubt on Berwone's 'reformation' here, in that 'his mockery of sophistication is sophisticated'. Professor Barber arrives at this conclussion via his thesis that saturnalia lies behind all comedy and especially that holiday festivity is the spring-board of LLL; MND; TN; and H1V.

[33]Baldassare Castiglione, *The Book of The Courtier,* tr. by Sir Thomas Hoby, Everyman's Library (London, New York, 1928, 1944), Book III, 190-191.

[34]*A Study of Love's Labour's Lost,* 102-136.

[35]As tr. by Hoby, 303. John Charles Nelson, *Renaissance Theory of Love* (New York, 1958), 117 translates Castiglione's triad as "sense, reason, intellect". Thus also the tr. by Leonard E. Opdyck (New York, 1929), but Friench Simpson's tr. (New York, 1959) keeps Hoby's "sense, reason, understanding."

[36]Cyrus Hoy, "*Love's Labour's Lost* and the Nature of Comedy," SQ, XIII (Winter, 1963), 31, 32 has a definition of comedy pertinent at this point, regarding the duality of man's nature applicable alike to comedy and to tragedy.

[37]Re-reading of *The Book of The Courtier,* especially Book I, on Language; Book III, on the Lady; and Book IV, on Love has materially influenced my conclusions in the part Berowne and Rosaline play in the comedy. Regrettably, I did not see the excellent essay on *Twelfth Night* in Barber, *Shakespeare's Festive Comedy,* 240-261 until after I had completed this study; see particularly the section called "Liberty Testing Courtesy", 248-255 for the invoking of the *corteziania* of Castiglione.

Date Due

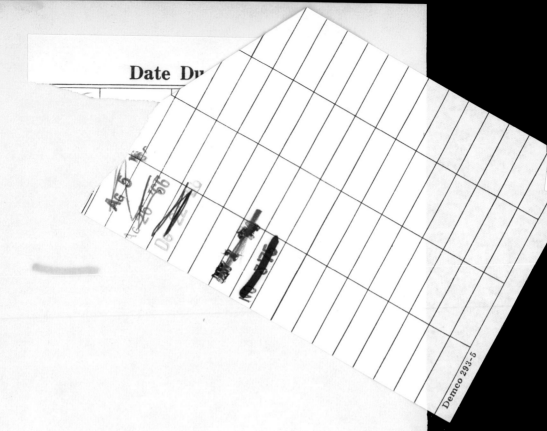

Demco 293-5

3 5282 00283 0688